CAN A SISTAH GET A LITTLE HELP?

CAN A SISTAH GET A LITTLE HELP?

Encouragement for Black Women in Ministry

TERESA L. FRY BROWN

THE PILGRIM PRESS
CLEVELAND

FOR Rev. Jesse Langston Boyd, Jr.,

ministry father in the cloud of witnesses,

and

for Tessie Bernice Ray Parks,

grandmother and griot

The Pilgrim Press, 700 Prospect Avenue, Cleveland, Ohio 44115-1100
thepilgrimpress.com
© 2008 Teresa L. Fry Brown

Printed in the United States of America on acid-free paper that contains post-consumer fiber.

13   12   11   5   4

Library of Congress Cataloging-in-Publication Data

Brown, Teresa L. Fry, 1951–
    Can a Sistah get a little help? : encouragement for black women in ministry / Teresa L. Fry Brown.
        p. cm.
    Includes bibliographical references.
    ISBN-13: 978-0-8298-1743-0 (alk. paper)
    1. African American women clergy.   2. Women in church work.
3. African Americans—Religion.   I. Title.
BR563.N4B675 2007
253.082—dc22   2007040374

CONTENTS

ACKNOWLEDGMENTS

I have been blessed to be surrounded by a multitude of spiritual and corporeal sistah mentors and mentees who have infused my life with prayer, nurture, guidance, support, and love. A host of sisters and brothers believed in me when I did not have the strength to believe in myself. It is said that "it is an ungrateful child who does not thank the ones who brought them across," and so I would like specifically to thank Reverend Sandra Blair, Reverend Rosetta Gadson, Reverend Kimberley Deathrage, Reverend Marie Davis, Reverend Darlene Smith, Reverend Zelia Harvey, Sister Carrie Dunson, and Sister Margaret Reese for reading this manuscript numerous times to make sure that others would understand and appreciate its content. Thank you for your push to help me finish. Thank you to all the women in ministry around the world who have asked for help and have freely given it to me. My daughter, Veronica Tinsley, is a special woman. She loves me enough to let me be different and still be "her only Mom." My love and appreciation go to my husband, Frank Brown, who makes space in our life together for me to be who God wants me to be.

PREFACE

"How did you do it?"

"What makes you keep going in spite of the obstacles?"

"Can you be my mentor?"

"How are we supposed to act, dress, love, live, worship, and counsel as women in ministry?"

"I am not a man. I do not look like a man. I do not want to be a man. How am I supposed to keep in touch with my femininity and be accepted as a minister?"

"What would you suggest to aid me in my ministry?"

"What good tools or resources are available to women in ministry?"

"How do you balance being a woman (and mother) and being in ministry?"

As I travel around the world and across the United States teaching and preaching, I am constantly asked these questions. Women confide in me that they discern little or no support from men (or often from women) of their God-called ministries, leaving them feeling alienated, abandoned, and sometimes perplexed. Support systems are few and far between. Role models for many are nothing more than a figment of their imagination. Most women would welcome having someone with whom to talk, to consider options, to commiserate, or just to share their joy uninhibited. The women entering ministry that I meet in the classroom have many of the same concerns I had when I began ministry some twenty-five years ago. I do not have all the answers, but I am able to draw on my personal journey to share successes and failures, joys and sorrows, disappointments and surprises, apprehensions and assurances of women in ministry. And sometimes that's enough.

Contemporary women are not the first to encounter resistance or even acceptance in their journey in ministry. Knowing how far we have come and how far we have to go is foundational to getting help. Listen to this:

> I did not speak much till I had reached my forty-second year, when it was revealed to me that the message that has been given to me I had not yet delivered, and the time had come. As I can read but little, I question within myself how it would be possible for me to deliver the message, why I did not understand the Scriptures. . . . Whilst I thus struggled, there seemed a light from heaven to fall upon me which banished all my desponding fears and I was enabled to form a new resolution. . . .[1]

These words are part of the call story of Elizabeth, the first recorded African American woman preacher. She was born a slave in 1766 and is said to have preached her first sermon in 1808 in Baltimore, Maryland. At age thirty she attended meetings in the vicinity of her home and, though urged to speak, she "shrank from it" due to her reverence for the cross. Elizabeth (no last name recorded) was forty-two at that time. She preached for more than fifty years in the Methodist Episcopal

---

1. Bettye Collier Thomas, *Daughters of Thunder: Black Women Preachers and Their Sermons, 1850–1979* (San Francisco: Jossey Bass, 1998), 226–27.

Church,[2] until she was ninety years old.[3] She preached about personal salvation and divine conversation with God.

Within the enslaved community, the Black preacher emerged as a central figure, one who inspired and gave hope. A few were privileged to engage in their tasks relatively freely; but most were watched closely as potentially dangerous sources of leadership and could be severely punished for the "wrong" kind of preaching. Confined to a White-approved message (or else double entendres) in public, Black preachers therefore came into their own in secret meetings, expressing hope for God's deliverance and freedom in this life as well as offering hope and consolation in heaven. Many Black preachers were skilled orators, using vivid biblical imagery and dramatic delivery in a lively service with free congregational response in shouting, music, and dance. Some preachers learned to read the Bible, especially in the earlier decades of the century, but even those who could not read knew their Bible well. Biblical imagery, along with influence from evangelical Protestant hymns and adaptation of African song, dance, and rhythmic patterns, produced one of the most distinctive forms of slave religion—the spiritual. Whatever their sources, spirituals gained form and identity in the Black experience, where they were communal and active. Subsequently scholars have debated their meaning, some emphasizing their protest and coded messages, others focusing on the religious elements of hope and consolation in suffering—ways for slaves to escape, albeit temporarily, the oppressive reality of their current existence.[4]

---

2. Collier-Thomas, *Daughters of Thunder,* 12–43.

3. Burt Loewenberg and Ruth Bogin, *Black Women in Nineteenth-Century American Life* (University Park: Pennsylvania State University Press, 1976), 127–30. See also Jean McMahon Humez, ed., "Documents: Female Preaching and the A.M.E. Church, 1820–1552," in *Gifts of Power: The Writings of Rebecca Jackson: Black Visionary, Shaker Eldress,* (Amherst: University of Massachusetts Press, 1931), 316-317.

4. Susan Hill Lindley, *You Have Stept Out of Your Place: A History of Women and Religion in America,* 1st ed. (Louisville, Ky.: Westminster John Knox Press, 1996), 175.

Though African women were mothers, priests, and queen mothers who served as keepers of the traditions and rituals, a stark feature of African American women's existence has been their invisibility, isolation, tokenism, and exclusion from societal privilege. Yet African American women have tried to move African Americans in general toward social equality through their religious traditions. In the sacred sphere, "church mothers" are pastors, evangelists, pastor's wives, missionaries, deaconesses, and leaders of organized women's religious groups. They have been the founders, administrators, teachers, and financial support for the Black church and community. These role models, power brokers, and venerable elders provide continuity and unity during transition and serve as a counter force to fragmentation in the community. These church and community mothers serve as guardians of African American tradition and guides for social change. Through an oral tradition, churched and unchurched Black women tell of the purpose, meaning, and importance of sociocultural events and serve as the connective tissue of the community and culture. They hand down religious and community beliefs as educators ("Each one, teach one"), leaders ("You can't lead where you won't go or teach what you don't know"), and businesswomen ("God bless the child that's got his own"). They are deemed "prophetic troublers" in the community, reminding children and adults of their heritage and possibilities.[5] Their spiritual core, that indescribable "something within" that the mothers and fathers of the faith used to sing about, is rooted in a sense that we "have to do it" for communal survival. What gave them the gumption to stand tall in such adverse circumstances?

5. Cheryl Townsend Gilkes, "Role of Church and Community Mothers: Ambivalent American Sexism or Fragmented Familyhood?" in *Journal of Feminist Studies in Religion* 2 (Spring 1986): 41–59; "'Some Mother's Son and Some Father's Daughter': Gender and Biblical Language in the Afro-Christian Worship Tradition," in *Shaping New Visions: Gender and Values in American Culture*, ed. Clarissa W. Atkinson, Constance H. Buchanan, and Margaret R. Miles (Ann Arbor: UMI Research Press, 1987), 73–95.

In their spiritual autobiographies, nineteenth-century women repeatedly drew on Joel 2:28–29 and 1 Corinthians 14:34–35 as biblical supports for their calls, to combat opposition, and to seek spiritual egalitarianism. They leaned heavily on biblical texts despite the oppressive ways the Bible was used against them and others.[6] Understanding biblical texts about God's Spirit being poured on all humanity to be a mandate from God to articulate and spread God's Word, their calls were evident by the obvious ways they exhibited spiritual anointing and gifting. Impelled and strengthened by such evidence, some of these nineteenth-century women left societal spaces such as homes, families, children, and husbands in order to preach. Yet now as then innumerable women, despite feeling called, opt not to enter ministry because of the lack of role models, pressure of ostracism, and lack of self-confidence.

Then as now, women who responded to their calls despite everything had to contend as well with arguments about the "feminization of the church," in which the lack of male participation in churches or religious communities was attributed to—and often blamed upon—women's presence and personalities, women such as them. In a 1921 article in the *A.M.E. Review,* the editor describes the crisis in an article titled "Silly Women Masquerading in the Name of Religion." He castigates women preachers as generally ignorant, public nuisances, grotesque caricatures, who "carry, ostentatiously, a Bible, and adorn themselves with crosses, crucifixes, rosettes, or badges. . . ." He charges women with being too loud, too conspicuous, and too visible, reminding his readers that women's work was to be with the poor or with children in the role of stewardess or deaconesses. For,

---

6. Chanta M. Haywood, "Prophesying Daughters: Nineteenth Century Black Religious Women, the Bible, and Black Literary History," in *African Americans and the Bible: Sacred Texts and Social Textures,* ed. Vincent Winbush (New York: Continuum, 2000), 355–61.

the horde of irresponsible "evangelists" and women in religious garb, bearing different names, are attaining such proportions that pastors should refuse to recognize them. . . . as a rule they can sing and are glib with a slangy harangue which may create a temporary attraction for the crowd.[7]

Apparently in an attempt to placate or perhaps silence these very women, the editor ends his comments by saying women have always had a place in the church as prophets, evangelists, and ministering saints. The implication is that women who work quietly in the background will be elevated for their good works while those who seek a more visible—and particularly, preaching—role are an embarrassment to the church.

In this the editor was apparently entrenched in the larger culture's ideology of true womanhood, which understood the domain of women as being the home—to be kept immaculately . . . for men, whose domain therefore was any area outside the home, including the church. Women instead were to be pure, chaste, and virginal, eternally available for the needs and pleasures of men. So although women were responsible for teaching men and children about faith,[8] for reading the Bible, leading prayers, and teaching religion in the home, they were castigated for doing so in public.

In the twenty-first century these very same beliefs and charges are typical. There are special conferences, programs, and ministries to "attract" men to the church—women purportedly having driven them away. Women are being denied ordination or their ministerial orders are being rescinded. In some denominations women are removed from lay leadership positions to make room for more men—a phenomenon I talk about as senior pastors "birthing baby boys and killing all the baby girls."

---

7. *A.M.E. Review*, 38, no. 2 (October 1921): 89.
8. Hill Lindley, *You Have Stept Out of Your Place*, 52–54.

Yet, though men have seen women's ability and felt threatened, women recognize such ability and celebrate it. Social historian Paula Giddings' research into the lives of Black women from slavery forward records the contributions of Black women in American social transformation. She writes that, when Black women define themselves, they are able to speak for themselves. Furthermore, through Black women's work with Black men, children, and the world to assure equality for all, they influence the destiny of the entire African American community. And while virtually voiceless in society except as teachers and members of the church, Black women have always had a voice in raising children—a significant, far-reaching role. Indeed, ordinary, everyday Black women have worked for transformation and the survival of the Black family, church, and community throughout the centuries of Black life in America.

So Black women have always had influence; the problem is that their gifts and influence have often not been officially recognized. Ordination is one such example. Denominational polity often does not sanction ordination of women or persons outside a particular family. If women founded denominations or if at that denomination's founding women were included equally, then typically the matter of their ordination was not in question. Yet even today political pressure within denominations that historically ordain women often leads to denial of ordination. Little wonder, then, that some women see no reason to get ordained because of the restrictions that come with ordination, which they know or feel may overshadow what God has called them to do.[9]

Such concerns are not new. Mark Chavis, in *Ordaining Women: Culture and Conflict in Religious Organizations,* ex-

---

9. See Teresa Fry Brown, *Weary Throats and New Songs: Black Women Proclaiming* (Nashville: Abingdon Press, 2003), for an extensive discussion of historical and contemporary Black women's call to ministry and the ordination process.

plores centuries-old beliefs, myths, folklore, and religiocultural affirmations concerning the ordination of women.[10] The arguments for and against the call to ministry and ordination of women are legion, and they typically begin with questions of biblical authority and creation order. Such arguments insist that women were created "second" from a man's rib and that this means God ordained men to be first in all things. Not wanting to dismiss women's usefulness, such positions often then purport that the "noblest" profession in the world is motherhood, a notion that either deliberately or by implication means that women who are not physically able to have children or choose not to do so are unemployed or misguided. There is more: women's minds are said to be too small to contain and fathom the ideology of ministry; they are said to be physically too weak for the rigors of ministry; and women who enter ministry are purported to be trying to impinge on "male" territory and destroy the very foundations of created order. The list goes on.

Yet there are other voices, too. Reinterpretation of biblical texts and their authority, such as through the 1898 publication of the *Women's Bible*, opens the way for all persons to be engaged in all forms of ministry. In such publications, women are said already to be in some form of ministry in hospitals, schools, homes, and community. Those people who validate the endowment of the Holy Spirit as verification of faith defer to a person's own testimony of God's anointing as ministerial ordination.

Traditional Black denominations and mainline Protestant denominational rule changes have provided somewhat different opportunities for women's ordination. Those traditional Black denominations that were formed in a move toward religious freedom show a long history of ordaining women. According to Chavis, the first two to affirm women's call were the National Baptist Convention and the Pentecostal Holiness Church, both

---

10. Mark Chavis, *Ordaining Women: Culture and Conflict in Religious Organizations* (Cambridge: Harvard University Press, 1997), 17.

in 1895. Black Methodists were not only hierarchical but also a bit slower and more divisive in affirming women's ordination. The African Methodist Episcopal Zion Church (A.M.E.Z.) initiated women's ordination in 1898, followed by the African Methodist Episcopal Church (A.M.E.), with deacons in 1948 and elders in 1960. Finally, the Christian Methodist Episcopal Church (C.M.E.) began full ordination of women in 1966.[11]

Concurring with Chavis, historian Bettye Collier Thomas documents that the African Methodist Episcopal Zion (A.M.E.Z.) was the first Black denomination to grant suffrage—or the right to vote and hold office in the church—to women in 1876. One such woman was Julia Foote, a nineteenth-century preaching woman in the Methodist Episcopal Church.[12] Late in life, she became the first woman ordained in the A.M.E.Z. Church. She struggled with the disparity of "church" teachings and how they were played out in reality in both church and society. She could not reconcile how persons who said that they believed in God could preach against Blacks as human beings.[13] In her spiritual narrative, *A Brand Plucked from the Fire*, Foote exemplifies the way Black women across history denied their calls—at least until they could no longer escape the moving of God's Spirit in their lives and the life of the church. Foote relates:

> When called of God, on a particular occasion, to a definite work, I said, "Lord, not me." Day by day I was more impressed that God would have me work in his vineyard. I thought it could not be that I was called to preach—I, so weak and ignorant. Still, I knew all things were possi-

11. Ibid., 16–17.
12. Julia Foote, *A Brand Plucked from the Fire: An Autobiographical Sketch* (Cleveland: Lauer & Yost, 1886), printed in *Spiritual Narratives*, ed. Henry Louis Gates Jr. (New York: Oxford University Press, 1988), 112.
13. Ibid., 9–21, 65.

ble with God, even to confounding the wise by foolish things of this earth. Yet, in me there was a shrinking. . . . I had always been opposed to the preaching of women, and had spoken against it, though, I acknowledge, without foundation. This rose before me like a mountain, and when I thought of the difficulties they had to encounter, both from professors and non-professors, I shrank back and cried, "Lord, I cannot go!"[14]

Foote, along with Mary J. Small, was ordained a deacon in 1894. However, when Small was ordained an elder in 1898, she apparently became a threat to male clergy, elders having the power and authority to supervise other clergy. In protest, other denominations maintained that the A.M.E.Z. had challenged the natural order of life by ordaining Small. Mary Small's husband, with whom she shared pastoral appointments, left the denomination to become a Colored (Christian) Methodist Episcopal (C.M.E.) due to untenable pressures from church authorities regarding his wife. The Christian Methodist Episcopal Church (C.M.E.) ordained women between 1895 and 1960, but there are few records of names and numbers. We do know that Mary Mims was made a C.M.E. elder in Kentucky in 1897.[15]

Although Florence Spearing Randolph was licensed to preach and was ordained a deacon and an elder in the late nineteenth century, her story is not all rosy. The African Methodist Episcopal Zion Church welcomed Reverend Spearing Randolph into full conference membership in 1898. She received appointments to several churches (against the wishes of her husband) between 1925 and 1946. She was assigned to a small congregation as supply pastor at Poughkeepsie, New York, and at Little Zion, Varick Memorial, New York, and subsequently as supply pastor to Summit, New Jersey, for twenty-

---

14. Ibid., 67.
15. Collier Thomas, *Daughters of Thunder*, 14–27.

one years. She worked diligently and the churches grew. As still happens today, it was not at all uncommon for women like her to be assigned to a "dead" church (or at least one on life support), where they were deliberately given little encouragement. When their leadership resulted in the church becoming healthy, they were often replaced—as was Spearing Randolph by a young man—and sent to another "dying" place. Through such machinations by the church authorities, Spearing Randolph worked as an itinerant pastor for fifty years.[16] Hers was one of the few sermon collections of a Black woman preacher of that era. Her sermons typically focused on sin, economic empowerment, racial discrimination, gender ideology, and women's capabilities in religious work.[17]

Other denominations were similarly reluctant and even devious in their stance toward women in ministry. Historian Collier Thomas lists the African Methodist Episcopal (A.M.E.) Church as first granting women the position of evangelist to avoid the ordination question. Sophie Murray was given that status at Mother Bethel A.M.E. in Philadelphia in 1816. Although opposed to ordaining women, male clergy welcomed such women evangelists because they built churches, raised funds, and ministered to the membership through church revivals, camp meetings, and, beginning in 1904, Women's Days.

The official debate about Black women's ordination began in the African Methodist Episcopal Church in the 1880s. Although Bishop Henry McNeal Turner ordained Sarah Ann Hughes in 1884, she was de-ordained in 1885 when Bishop Turner was sanctioned.[18] However, the "Church of Allen," representative of the liberation movement of African American religious institutions in America, moved with "all deliberate (integrationist) speed"' in its ordination and advancement of women.

---

16. Chavis, *Ordaining Women*, 6–17, 24–27.
17. Ibid., 26, 33.
18. Collier Thomas, *Daughters of Thunder*, 14–27.

Sixty-three years after Hughes' ordination trauma, the A.M.E. Church sanctioned women as Local Deacons. Now as then, Local Deacons are assigned to a specific church for the duration of their ministry where they are supervised by the senior pastor who is generally an Itinerant Elder. Local Deacons must seek permission to participate in marriages, funerals, and outside preaching engagements. In 1948, Rebecca M. Glover was ordained as such a Local Deacon and served as assistant pastor of Metropolitan African Methodist Episcopal in Washington, D.C. She received full ordination in the A.M.E. Church in 1956 when women began to be ordained as Local Elders. Women like Glover were to work at a designated church but had full ministry rights. Four years later, A.M.E. women were ordained as Itinerant Elders with authority to be assigned to any church as pastor or associate pastor. The ranks of supervisory pastor or presiding elder opened to them in 1973. At the A.M.E. General Conference held in Cincinnati in 1964, the Rev. Carrie T. Hooper became the first woman to run for bishop. One hundred fifteen years after Sarah Hughes encountered prejudice in the General Conference, Vashti Murphy McKenzie was elected as a bishop of the church, followed in 2004 by the election of Sarah Davis and Carolyn Tyler Guidry. Visionary women ran for episcopal office over the years to "keep the door open," ready to expunge the excuse that there were no women available for the position. They faced castigation, cruel jokes, punishment on the local level, and at times minimal support from other women.

While many traditional Black denominations' struggles with biblical authority and gender bias resulted in ordination of women, several denominations continued to resist. The Church of God in Christ (COGIC), for example, did not ordain women as elders, pastors, or bishops. Although officially this was because while women were allowed to teach only men could preach, in fact the public speaking of prominent women in the denomination is indistinguishable from male preaching.

Women creatively established alternative venues for proclamation of God's word without benefit of ordination. The most powerful women's department in nineteenth-century Black denominations was located in the Church of God in Christ. When denied pastoral positions, the women became evangelists. They led churches in the absence or death of the pastor and developed individual congregations. COGIC women who began churches were included in the church history. They assumed leadership in education, prayer, and Bible study and sustained the churches economically.[19]

Their example is one instance of the many Black women who were nontraditionalists. They developed innovative ways of worshiping and working without totally disregarding established patterns they nevertheless found oppressive and restrictive. One such nontraditionalist was Mother Leafy Anderson, who founded the first African American spiritual church in the 1920s in New Orleans. She practiced a blend of Roman Catholicism, African American Protestantism, Holiness, Pentecostalism, nineteenth-century spiritualism, and African-based religion such as Voodoo. Such spiritual churches in New Orleans offered ordination to women's leaders as evangelists, ministers, bishops, and even archbishops.[20]

Black women from the nineteenth century until the present have thus sought to avoid "perpetual pregnancies" by finding alternative means to describe and proclaim their faith. In spite of social barriers and denominational harassment, they have used their faith to critique and challenge the status quo, seek liberation from marginalization, oppression, discrimination, and violence, seek freedom for self-definition, self-affirmation, and

19. Cheryl Townsend Gilkes, "Together in the Harness: Women's Tradition in the Sanctified Church," in *If It Wasn't for the Women* (Maryknoll, N.Y.: Orbis, 2001), 48–54.
20. Catherine Wessinger, *Religious Institutions and Women's Leadership: New Roles inside the Mainstream* (Columbia: University of South Carolina Press, 1996), 363, 373, 378, 381.

self-determination—in short, to live out their calls. Historian Darlene Clark Hine describes a *culture of dissemblance* in which Black women developed "the appearance of openness and disclosure but actually shield[ed] the truth of their inner lives and selves from oppressors" to counteract negative social and sexual images of their womanhood.[21] Delores Carpenter in *A Time for Honor: A Portrait of African American Clergywomen*, lists eleven factors that inhibit African American women from moving forward in ministry: sexism, male clergy, racism, female laity, lack of leadership skills, weak interpersonal skills, lack of mentors, male laity, weak oratorical skills, lack of advocacy, and lack of family support.[22] Each of these is painfully relevant in the lives of Black women who seek to do God's work. In my experience some women at times coyly feign adoption of domesticated, subservient, less intelligent demeanors while working out their calls. Others stand defiantly in their own personhood, allowing God to open the way for their calls. In the twenty-first century, Black women continue the creative process of establishing new denominations, finding ways of being faithful to their calls.

How did Black women understand their calls? And how did others write of it? In *The Burdensome Joy of Preaching*, homiletician James Earle Massey states that a call is the conviction of God's claim on one's life, which leads to a sense of focused identity and integration of the self for action, harnessed energies, and heightened creativity. In contrast to call, he suggests that anointing gives a person a sense of being identified with God's will in relating to some need, assertiveness to act, and an "instinct" for relating to what needs to be done. Going further,

---

21. Darlene Clark Hine, Elisa Barkley Brown, and Rosalyn Terborg-Penn, eds., *Black Women in America: An Historical Encyclopedia, Vol. 1* (Bloomington and Indianapolis: Indiana University Press, 1993), 15.
22. Delores Carpenter, *A Time for Honor: A Portrait of African American Clergywomen* (St. Louis, Mo.: Chalice Press, 2001), 116.

Massey then delineates three types of authority by which we proclaim God's word: derived authority is our God-given right to preach (Rom. 10:15); shared authority is dispensed in a spiritual community where credentials are given to authorized [ordained] persons, endorsed and accountable to a community or heritage; and finally, authority can be given to us as a result of spiritual experience through observable evidence of a character, wisdom, and a contagiously God-oriented life.[23]

Liturgical theologian Carol Noren offers another perspective, blending research on historical and contemporary women to outline the process of a call to ministry. She begins by citing how women tend to identify their sense of ministerial vocation. Such identification may be complicated by a woman's uncertainty or subsequent tension in relationship to the church and institutional support of the call, for women who respond to a divine ministerial call are often viewed as difficult, divisive, different, caustic, crazy, or controversial depending on the history of women in ministry in a particular denomination or local church structure. There are spiritual narratives and biographical statements of women's call as being both life-changing and crisis-oriented. Noren's historical research shows that women have spent an inordinate amount of time appealing to men's sense of justice or fairness in "allowing them to become part of the clergy." Such need for permission from (usually) men leads Noren to describe the ordination process as being basically a professional credentialing vehicle. She suggests that nowadays denominations look for outward evidence of a call rather than or at least in addition to an inward manifestation. Thus we see how call has become simply a sense of vocation rather than a divine mandate for ministry.[24]

---

23. James Earle Massey, *The Burdensome Joy of Preaching* (Nashville: Abingdon Press), 1998, 25–46.

24. Carol Noren, *Woman in the Pulpit* (Nashville: Abingdon Press, 1992), 15–29.

My journey in ministry, as well as those of many of my sister reverends, has included several of the experiences and understandings Noren notes. Until my early thirties, I worked in Black Baptist churches as a choir member and director, Sunday school superintendent, Bible study teacher, missionary, director of women's ministry, youth director, secretary, cook, counselor, and community activist. I felt at home in the company of other sisters and brothers who also had dedicated their lives to working in God's vineyard. With the exception of my great aunt and one or two other women, I did not witness women in ordained or pulpit ministry. In fact, the tasks I have listed were not called "real ministry" but "women's ministry." I understood the importance of each service or task to the total church program. Everyone had a place and there was a place for everyone. Although the churches I attended were composed of 70–95 percent women, the titular leadership was and had always been male. As a young woman I was told that the kinds of ministries in which I was involved were the only options for women in the church because the "Bible says" women are to be silent in church due to Eve's sin.

Called into ordained ministry at age thirty-two, I was told to wait until the senior pastor figured out what to do with me. I had to shift paradigms and think about why God was directing me into a "man's world" and what I was to do there. At that time there were few female role models, no female mentors, and only distant sisters with whom to share this strange world. My family life was upended. My social life dried up. Men thought that I was no longer feminine, that I was trying to be a male, or that I had sexual identity problems. Women saw me as a threat to their positions in the church, their relationships with the senior pastor, their role definition for women, and their own sense of success or failure. With such lack of encouragement, was it surprising that I thought I had lost my mind? Why was God "bothering" me? I was happy being a church worker, political activist, and mother. All I wanted to do was go to church, sing in the choir, and raise my child.

Twenty-two years ago the late Rev. Dr. Praitha Hall preached, "Faith is not faith until it is tested in the crucible of struggle and the fiery trials of life."[25] This renowned pastor, preacher, professor, and civil rights leader became my first female preaching mentor and role model, my light from heaven. As I struggled both with questioning why God would call me and with navigating the political waters and finding my voice, I heard her say that to refuse to preach or be refused the right to preach is like being "perpetually pregnant." Having had a child, I knew that the last thing I wanted to do was to be perpetually pregnant. Regardless of the emotional effects of and talk about my divorce, regardless of the verbal attacks by women and political threats by men in the church, regardless of being alienated from some family members, and regardless of my own self-doubt, I understood then that I had no choice but to give birth to God's word. Praitha Hall's oft-repeated statement about faith not being faith until it is tested in the crucible of struggle and fiery trials of life became a mantra for my journey in ministry. Now, finally I could say, "I stood in the total authenticity of my being—Black, preacher, Baptist, woman. For the same God who made me a preacher, made me a woman. And, I am convinced that God was not confused on either count."[26]

In the course of twenty-five years I have learned that the ministry in which I was engaged for most of my life is the same ministry I am doing now. The difference is the title that accompanies my work. I am a Black woman, wife, mother, daughter, sister, friend, ordained minister, seminary professor, womanist scholar, student advisor, and community activist. I am also a representative of women in ministry on several levels, mentoring women contemplating, entering, or already in ordained ministry as well as women who are active in lay ministries in the local church.

---

25. Praitha Hall, Chicago Sunday Evening Club, 30 Good Minutes, "When Faith Trembles," program #4318, February 6, 2000.
26. Praitha Hall, quoted in Joy Bennett Kinnon, "Live Well—Wear Your Own Shoes," Sisterspeak interview, *Ebony* (Nov. 2002).

I am amazed that even at the beginning of the twenty-first century there are still many women perpetually pregnant, waiting to deliver the proclamation to which they are called. The pains of postponed birth lead to toxic lives, lives at times filled with self-loathing, mistrust of others, alienation from family, disdain for the institutional church, and a sense that these women are the butt of some cruel cosmic joke. They seek to birth their ministries before the Word and work are aborted. Of course, some women may be complicit in their perpetual pregnancy. Some have been their own worst enemy by listening to old "tapes" in their heads about how they ought to live out their femininity, how they are acting like men, how they are taking power away from men, how they are afraid of men's critique. Some listen to old tapes of sister stuff that blocks the call of God; some hesitate, afraid of losing their current status. These are just a few of the reasons women do not answer the call to preach.

Opposition to women's proclamation arises from—as well as themselves—the most unexpected sources. Men bear the burden of blame most of the time because of historical opposition. But it is surprising that women often overlook the barriers regarding women's leadership and ordination that are erected by other women. Naysayers are often other women. And, as occurred historically, denominational decision makers still deliberately assign a woman to a "dead" church or one on life support, then when the church has been revivied, re-assign a male pastor, and the woman is sent to another "dying" place.[27] There are times such as these when women do the work but receive little praise. Their creative and daring delivery is not acknowledged, let alone celebrated; indeed, their productivity is often credited to the male successors.

Another group of women pastors chooses to align themselves with the hegemonic forces that admit a select few women as long as they act and dress the part of a head-nodding-

---

27. Chavis, *Ordaining Women*, 6–17, 24–27.

dressed-to-the-nines-appendage-to-a-man's ministry. They refuse to work to admit other women to this leadership "club" because being the "first and only" is a privilege and they need no
competition. Some pick up the habits of their handlers, refusing
to acknowledge that it is God and not humans who call preachers. They proclaim the word of God according to the latest messiah's gospel as they cautiously walk the party line.

Some women leave one denomination that refuses them ordination and affiliate with one that does. Some women are ordained for a particular purpose other than pastoring. Many
women operate without institutional ordination yet find ways to
lead congregations. There is another group that preaches "by
any means necessary." These women creatively find ways to live
out their ministries if necessary without anyone else's approval.
They negotiate the pain of giving birth at times without prena-
tal care or midwives. They affirm that all ground is holy. They
are not limited to proclaiming God's word in traditional settings
or traditional ways. They dare to deliver the word regardless of
the size of the congregation, number of engagements, place of
ministry, approval rating, human imposed barriers, ostracism by
their sisters or brothers, or financial report.

THIS BOOK'S PURPOSE

My focus is how Black women may faithfully continue to navigate the internal and external challenges of ministry. The bulk
of this book is based on my twenty-two years in ordained ministry and as a seminary professor, during which I have learned
that, with a set of cultural coping mechanisms and values,
African American women can not only survive but thrive as
leaders and mentors in spite of the brick ceiling. These needed
coping mechanisms and values are:

1. survival skills
2. network/support systems
3. work ethic

4. mentors and sponsors

5. a sense of self-worth and self-confidence

6. spiritual values

7. balance in life

8. leadership style

9. cultural identity[28]

These are transmitted by Black families through direct teaching examples, assigned tasks, and negative examples and life stories of what happens when one ignores their relevance. I provide a fuller explanation of each of these coping mechanisms or values in my first book, *God Don't Like Ugly: African American Women Handing on Spiritual Values*, but you will also find these values woven throughout this book's chapters. Alongside these, I engage personal experience, conversations with women in ministry over the past thirty or so years, concerns of seminary students, events in local church women's ministries, ecclesial concerns and actions for women in ministry, and scholarly insights.

As preparation for this book, I have conversed with approximately two hundred ordained and 450 lay women in ministry about the issues most relevant to them. The refrain of "Make sure you tell them about . . ." punctuated each conversation. I also travel extensively presenting at women's conferences or women's days or weekends. In sessions or over meals, I am routinely asked things such as: How did you survive in ministry? How do you handle your "power"? Aren't you afraid? What would you recommend for the next generation of women preachers? Would you be my mentor? How do you balance all you do? So in the pages that follow I discuss lessons learned and lessons to be learned during a journey to self-empowerment in ministry. You who are reading

---

28. Teresa Fry Brown, *God Don't Like Ugly: African American Women Handing on Spiritual Values* (Nashville: Abingdon Press, 2000), 50–52, 81–83.

my book I imagine as being lay and clergy women in ministry and in a whole range of women's ministry departments, seminaries, departments of religion, and women's studies departments.

I have written this book of my journey in ministry as a Black woman primarily for Black women—though I realize that the discussions are applicable to most women in ministry regardless of ordination status, denominational affiliation, age, or ethnicity. Each chapter takes the form of remembrances, vignettes, or discussions interwoven with common concerns raised by Black women in ministry who contact me via e-mail, at conferences, in church, by phone, and in face-to-face conversations. I am well aware that there are those who encountered no roadblocks or discernable prejudices in living out their call and so what follows is not meant to be definitive of all experiences of women in ministry.

In this journey, my sisterhood of Black reverend sister friends has been the incubator for contemporary "Mother Wit" (common sense sayings), "Sistah Sense" (my words for the kind of problem solving Black women do based on in-the-moment experiences or more often lived experiences—problem solving like putting tape on a run in pantyhose because you don't have another pair handy and you are about to enter the pulpit), and truisms, musings, and lessons they never tell you in seminary or the church about how women can lead self-loving, self-sufficient, and self-controlled lives. Each chapter includes survival suggestions we have learned on our individual and collective journeys.

OUTLINE OF CHAPTERS

In chapter 1, "I Think I'm Going Out of My Head," I discuss the significance of the "call" to ministry, authority issues, and contemporary affirmation and discouragement of women in ministry: what the personal impact of the "call" on all aspects of one's life is; how one might deal with discouragement or denial of a call into ministry; obstacles to ministry in the absence of female role models or support systems; fear of male authority; what I call " sexual surrogacy," "first lady syndrome," and "pantry mentality"; and ways in which one's past may abort one's future in ministry.

The second chapter, "Express Yourself," reviews questions and concerns about a woman "looking the part" in ministry. It focuses on the importance of a woman's voice, silence, presence, carriage, sexuality, deportment, ministerial dress, self-assertion, self-acceptance, and self-critique, as well as ways to challenge or comply with authorities. How, in short, can one remain female in a male world? I expand on my concept of *in*-powerment (ascribed characteristics based on power disparities) versus *em*powerment (tapping the power of one's own mind and spirit) grounded in self-development, self-resilience, self-reliance, and self-naming.

In the third chapter, "Hormonal Shifts," I demystify the view that women's crying should be equated with emotional, mental, spiritual, and physical weakness. I attend to issues of burnout, Sabbath, managing emotions, health, illness, self-care, spirituality, and contemplative life. I discuss such questions as Can real preachers be pregnant or menstruate? How do women in ministry mange self-care? How can we balance being a mythical "superwoman" with being a real woman? When is multitasking an excuse for avoiding an issue or an ineffective use of our time? If we die tomorrow from overwork, who takes our place? Will anyone really care?

In chapter 4, "Stumbling Blocks and Safety Nets," I consider the importance of and cost to family and friends of being an intimate support system, looking at matters such as being single, marriage, divorce, remarriage, widowhood, child care, preacher's kids, and so forth. I assess perceptions of women in ministry, stereotypical family roles, the toll of ministry on family members, and families' involvement in ministry. How does the support or lack of support from a spouse affect one's ministry? What is the impact of changes in senior pastor leadership? How do geographical location, age, changes in marital status, family configuration, denomination, or ministry style affect how a woman is accepted in ministry?

The fifth chapter, "No Woman Is an Island," delineates mentoring configurations and fortitude, as well as networking, toxic alliances, and affected support. How does one choose or disengage a ministry mentor; build viable ministry associations; and find support systems for moving past hurt, confusion, or embarrassment? What are some ways to share the acceptance, information, and promotion that comes with ministry?

In chapter 6, "Carving Out Your Own Space," I discuss the advantages and necessity of education—distance learning, seminary, Bible college, and self study, as well as credentialing and degree acquisition. I also survey how women's ministry and women are presented and valued in books on ministry, as well as on tapes, CDs and DVDs, and in specialized ministry programs and leadership models. How true is it for Black women that "Your gifts will make room for you?" Finally, I explore alternative ways of doing ministry, such as copastoring, social activism, conference preaching, being on the circuit, revivals, evangelism, chaplaincy, teaching, music, and web ministries.

The seventh chapter, "Swimming with Sharks but Safely Reaching the Shore," focuses on how to navigate religious-political systems and their dangers, such as sexual harassment, age discrimination, physical prejudices, token program participation, pastoral appointments, and submission. I discuss the reality of the "clean-up woman" (Betty Wright), "the first and only" and the "exception to the rule" syndromes, as well as suggesting some ways to transformation through prophetic engagement. What happens when a sister gives you the wrong tools and shows up at your funeral to gloat?

In the epilogue, "Sister Help," I summarize the mentoring lessons and look forward to what is yet to be learned. I ponder the question that our foremother, Maria Stewart, one of the earliest female public speakers in the United States, raised in 1832: "How long shall the fair daughters of Africa be compelled to bury their minds and talents beneath a load of iron pots and kettles?"[29] This became the rallying cry for nineteenth-century Black women to stand up for themselves, unite with other women, and fight for equality. Twenty-first century Black women ministers must answer this question for themselves as they seek to conquer their ministerial mountains.

The book is prompted by and reflects conversations I have had over the decades with women in ministry, those contemplating ministry, those new to ministry, and seasoned women in ministry. I have been blessed to have developed a God-ordained circle of sisters over the years who have provided just the help I needed at the right (and sometime, not the right but eventual) time, and who help me sing "How I Got Over" when all looks lost. In addition, I have been given a group of brothers in ministry who have been that other voice I needed to take the next step or who watch my back so I can run on a little further. Innumerable congregations of saints (and some "ain'ts") have responded when I asked verbally or nonverbally, "Can a sistah get a little help?"

My grandmother's favorite song is "If I Can Help Somebody," which declares that if we do not extend ourselves for the benefit of others our lives will be meaningless. When this sister needs a little help deciphering and accepting the burdens and blessings of my call, I listen for the myriad voices of my reverend sister-friends, that cloud of witnesses, those women who walked the path before me, women who are walking this path with me, and women who will walk it after me. I know I am not alone. There are many lessons we have learned and taught each other, just as there are lessons yet to be taught or learned in sometimes painful, sometimes humorous conversations in which we deconstruct and reconstruct the authenticity of our calls. When I am finished with this ministerial journey, I would like to remember that I gave all my sisters and my brothers a little help. After all, someone helped me.

---

29. Marilyn Richardson, ed., *Maria W. Stewart, America's First Black Woman Political Writer* (Bloomington: Indiana University Press, 1987), 38.

ONE

·

I THINK
I'M GOING OUT
OF MY HEAD

·

Hello,

This is Teresa Fry Brown. I met you at that conference last year in Atlanta. You probably don't remember but you asked me to pray for you. You were going through something at your home church having to do with you sensing a call to ministry. Well, I was just sitting here working on my syllabus for the fall and thought about how many women ask me to pray for them concerning the "call." Probably they think that because I have been doing this for a while I have some quick fix for the hell that women go through trying to do God's work. Well, I do not have a magic answer—because every woman's experience is different. But I can provide little snippets of encouragement, if you have a few minutes. I hope it helps you.

I have taught "Women and Preaching" since 1996 at Candler School of Theology at Emory University in Atlanta, Georgia. In each class we debate the issue of women in ministry. The purpose of the assignment is to raise the question so that women will be better equipped to stand in their calls and that men will know the reality of the prejudicial barriers women face in the institutionalized church.

I had an opportunity to test this pedagogical tool outside of the classroom in the summer of 2006. The assignment was a debate called "Women to Preach or Not to Preach?" The verbal combatants were fifty adolescents ages sixteen to eighteen at a summer theology camp in Georgia. I had had no prior contact with the group. I simply asked them to argue an assigned point regardless of their personal views. I randomly divided them into mixed gender groups, with their choice of a designated group reporter. After a fifteen-minute conferral period, they took to the microphone to expound on their beliefs concerning the role of women in ministry. Their responses showed me that the more things change the more they remain the same. Their arguments against women in ministry (preachers) were as follows:

- In the Bible, I think in Deuteronomy, it says that women must bow down to men.
- 1 Corinthians 11:8–9 states man is not from woman but woman from man.
- Woman was created to cater to all of man's needs.
- Men are the most powerful and prudent.
- Men should not listen to women.
- 2 Timothy 2:12 says women are not to preach or have authority but to be silent.
- All the prophets were males.
- In historical days men were pastors and preachers.
- The father is supposed to be the head of the household.
- Men do all the work anyway so they are also supposed to run the church.

The arguments in favor of women in ministry (preachers) were:

- Women are equal to men.
- They are called in the Word of God just like men.
- They are called to preach, teach, and do whatever God says.
- Women have a different point of view that is just as important as men's.
- Mary Magdalene was the one who told the men about Jesus' resurrection.
- Where do you come from?
- The woman is the giver of life and sometimes says things better than men.
- Women are more sensitive and can reach more sensitive spots in people.
- We need to see past all that strength stuff.
- God is the one who calls people to preach.
- There are more men on television with flashy reputations and stuff.
- Women can help more people.

Following the debate, I asked for other comments from the floor. My one request was they would listen objectively, and, in the words of one of my mentors, Dr. Jacqueline Grant, "hear each other into speaking." By this is meant allowing persons to voice an opinion, listen critically, and instead of vocally condemning a different opinion accept that everyone is entitled to his or her own thoughts. It is a way of honoring the humanity of the other and ending oppressive silences and dominating presences.

One young man pointedly said he was tired of women thinking they could tell men anything. He wanted women just to shut up. Another person said that she also thought only men should lead because women are weak and need someone to protect them. Another said that she had women who were preachers in her church and she saw nothing wrong with it. One young woman said the debate helped her understand that it was alright for her to speak in church.

Some of the group members groaned at the statements. Some whispered to the person sitting nearest. Some became animated with facial contortions and hand waving. Some quickly tried to locate a verse in their Bibles for confirmation. Some sat stoically either bored with the entire debate or thinking through the issue.

I found the young people's responses at the same time amazing and troubling. If this generation as a whole believes these statements, women will never find equity in the church in my lifetime, I thought. After a brief moment of grief I remembered there is always hope for change regardless of what negative forces are present.

Although their debate was brief, the young people entered into the centuries' old discussion of women's call to ministry. Someone in their brief lives had impregnated them with a stance on the issue, even though many of them had had little contact with women preachers.

Because it is still such a live issue, I revisit my personal "call" and the arguments against it every other month or so. I try to focus on the victories rather than the intermittent defeats, and sometimes I am successful. I even begin each sermon with "When I think of the goodness of Jesus and all he's done for me . . ." as a means of moving negativity out of my head before I expound on a word for which some are thirstily waiting—though others are merely tolerating it, anxious for me to finish. I find that whenever I am fatigued from the work of breaking down barriers, charting new pathways, defending my profession, or interceding for other women, I begin to question my own sanity for engaging in this mysterious profession we call ministry.

In my childhood a soul music group named Little Anthony and the Imperials sang "Going Out of My Head." Dionne Warwick's passionate arrangement resonated throughout my young adulthood. The song is a melodic expression of a person still so in love with another who no longer cares for her that she cannot conceive of being in any other relationship. The soloist is embroiled in the height of emotional and almost spiritual frustration. She cries incessantly. She is unable to formulate clear thoughts. Her passionate plea is to be noticed, wanted, and desired. She even blames herself for the alienation. She is a nonentity in the eyes of her beloved. The object of her affection is visible yet invisible. She thinks that she is losing her mind.

There have been times in my ministry that I felt this same way. I often ask myself what bit of insanity urges me to pursue the depths of an often unrequited love of ministry. Yes, I understand the love of Jesus, Jesus' sacrifice for my liberty, and the moral obligation to do what God says I should do. But that does not comfort me when I think I am going out of my head. In those moments, days, weeks, and months I long for the times when I could go anywhere, do anything, say anything, dress any way, converse with anyone, or openly purchase anything I wanted without sensing a pair of eyes judging me, without mocking voices saying "I knew she wasn't called" echoing in my ears. I become restless, angry, depressed, confused, and exhausted, and I basically resign myself to sitting for hours on my chaise lounge with a spoon and a half-gallon container of white chocolate raspberry ice cream and some green tea. In my head I ask repeatedly, "Why in the world would a God who is supposed to love me in spite of myself put this crazy burden of ministry on me? I must have done something wrong. Is this punishment? Well, I would think God could come up with something better than this."

After a sufficient time in my self-planned, self-invited "I do not want to do ministry ever, ever, ever again, not in this or any other life don't ask me to do anything again God has forgotten my address" pity party, I begin to think about God's action in my life. Just when I've decided I'll never go back to church, school, or even a family gathering, God whispers in my spiritual ears: "Didn't I promise I would go with you? Have I ever lied to you?

Come on, Teresa Lynn, get it together; let's go!" I engage in this spiritual verbal exchange for a while, including some words that only God can stand. Then I put aside my comfort food, take a bath, fix my hair, and sing a chorus of Chaka Khan's arrangement of "I'm Every Woman," Andre Crouch's "Through It All," or Kurt Carr's "For Every Mountain." Let me be clear: this occurred not only at the beginning of my years of ministry. It continues even now with regularity, particularly when it seems that life is passing me by, people critique my presence in ministry, or all the doors seem to be stuck. Perhaps you have engaged in similar battles.

The voices of doubt are evident in deafening assertions and in stifled murmurs, "Women are not supposed to preach," "She's trying to be a man," "What does her husband think?" "Child, I remember when she was in the choir," "That's why she can't get a man: she's got to run everything," "She going straight to hell, going against God," "Can't no woman tell me anything; all they do is run their mouths." "She might be able to preach but she can't pastor," or something similar. You fill in the particulars. It seems everyone has an opinion about women in ministry but few confront the call of a man or his actions and ministerial gifts following ordination. Male authority is seemingly equated to absolute, above question authority. Women, on the other hand, are thought to need male validation to decide everything from the color of their hair to appropriate times for menstruation and childbirth. The perennial theologically and socially ideal woman was created to take direction from a man and supply all his needs. She is pure, virtuous, and without blemish. She raises as many children as her spouse requires. She is the property of the male. She works nonstop, sunup to sundown, with little or no rest. She is described as a "helpmate," an aforethought, a subordinate, a lesser partner, an inferior, ready to please. She never has a negative thing to say about anything or anybody even when she is oppressed or abused. She has little or no brain of her own so she has no opinion worth considering. She keeps the man's castle and makes sure he is never lonely or depressed. If he is not religious, it is her fault. If he is unfaithful to her, it is her fault. If he is sick, it is her duty to make him well, just like his mother did. Any deviation from this model is unnatural, particularly in the house of God. "God is a man, after all. My Bible says that man is the head of the household; women are to be silent and let the man (who was made in God's image first and foremost) talk."

These comments and searing critiques permeate discussions of women in ministry in the preaching classes and seminars I teach. I have encountered countless students whose goal in life it is to emulate the latest preaching superstar rather than using the voice God gave them. They seem to believe that if they sound, look, act, dress, or preach like someone else, their ministry will be accepted. I suppose I should be honored that Martin Luther King, Juanita Bynum, Joyce Meyers, John Hagee, Barbara Brown Taylor, Rod Parsley, Eddie Long, Joel Osteen, T. D. Jakes, Paul Morton, Noel Jones, and Paula White regularly "enroll" in my classes. Yet I wonder why these students don't instead imitate Jesus' preaching style and delivery. I realize he had a small following compared to the often imitated contemporary voices, but I wonder anyway. Furthermore, I ponder how many live out for others their message's content and intent, including that crucifixion thing. Somehow I would rather the "sound-alikes" would just preach as themselves.

Excuse me, but I digress, as I often do.

As I was saying, I try to spend a couple of hours a day reviewing news stories about ministers and their self-named ministries and viewing televised or webcast sermonic presentations. Recently as I channel surfed, I tried to pay attention to a young male "megachurch" pastor/televangelist on one of the religious broadcasting channels. I have come to the conclusion that anyone who says he or she has cash, credentials (even if they are made up), an "anointed" calling, and, most important, "the right circuit" connections can be on television and most assuredly on

the Internet. Well, this young male preacher has a large following of new Christians who have felt disenfranchised from the
"traditional" church. I prayed that he would not say anything
that would make me angry. I certainly do not regard myself as
the sole voice of preaching, but I do know what is theologically
incorrect and what is prejudice cloaked in religion.

I watched the young man wax eloquent about his faith for
about five minutes. I thought, okay, everyone has different experiences. He is using his gifts to share the beauty of faith with
others. He leaned forward, looked directly in the camera, ad-
justed his tie, and changed the timbre of his voice. He tightened
his grip on the microphone, sweat pouring from his brow, and
went for the spiritual jugular. He cast his hook and reeled in the
spiritually expectant audience. He passionately proclaimed,
"The mother's blood never enters the baby, only the father's. . . .
That is why you do a paternity test to see who the father is. The
mother has nothing to do with who the child becomes." He went
on to parallel a believer's relationship with "God the Father"
through a spiritual paternity test and the place of men and
women in faith development. First my soul cringed, then I ex-
ploded. "I don't believe this! Where in the world did that come
from? Where did he study? Basic biology would teach you better than that."

Once upon a time I taught anatomy, physiology, neurology,
and endocrinology to undergraduates as the director of the
speech and hearing clinic at a midwestern university, so I know
more than many about the human developmental process. My
response was thus more than righteous indignation or a
homiletics teacher's analysis. To my utter horror, women in the
audience were agreeing, applauding, and praising God for
men's blood. They were so caught up that they were validating
women's subordination in front of God and everyone. Not only
was there a gross misrepresentation of the pregnancy and birth
process, but the program was being viewed worldwide and the
message was received as the gospel truth. The message was that

men (after all God is a man) determine life and identity. Women are just the incubation pods. Unfortunately, this belief system often carries over into the life of the church. Women are made to do grunt work, but what is considered the important work of the church is carried out by men. When we consider that in both historical and contemporary Black churches women comprised 75–95 percent of the membership, the harsh reality, the uncomfortable truth is that many of the deafening and murmuring voices against the presence of women in ministry are other women.

The incessant tape of the *"human call determinants"*— those who make it their life calling to decide who is worthy to be called by God—seems stuck on repeat. I would be lying if I said that I am perfect, never have an unholy thought, or have been some saintly person all of my life. I have things that I haven't told anyone but God, but I am proud of most of my life. When the thoughts of ministerial self-doubt begin to run through my head late at night when I am writing or when I am returning from an engagement, I find myself weeping as I look back over my life and wonder why God called me. I am grateful for the opportunity and know it did not have to happen. My adult daughter, Veronica, often chides me. "Mom, you can be your own worst enemy. You do not sufficiently appreciate who you are. You need to begin to demand that people recognize all that you are. God called you to do what you do and that should be enough." That little kick gets me started on the right track again.

Contemporary women in ministry are not the first and will most likely not be the last to encounter questions about the veracity of their call. I generally assign students in the "Women and Preaching" class or in women's ministry seminars the task of interviewing a woman who has been in active ministry at least fifteen years longer than themselves. They are to ask the woman about her call story, her journey in ministry, her family support, and if she is willing to offer a suggestion of how the student might live out his or her own call.

For example, my grandmother has been an active church woman for more than ninety years. She has served as a missionary, choir member, vacation Bible school and Sunday school teacher, cook, deaconess, and mother of the church. Her sister has been in ministry and served as pastor of a church for more than fifty years. Both were raised in a traditional African American household with ascribed gender roles. They were taught "proper" women's dress and mannerisms. Both knew their place and each chose to step out of that traditional place when she deemed it necessary. Both had long marriages and several children. They loved and respected their husbands until death. They navigated the competing demands of home and job as independent Black women. They supported the efforts of younger women, whether their choices were to tend a traditional home and family or pursue a nontraditional single adulthood and secular career.

When I answered my call to ministry I asked my grandmother what she thought. She said I had to do what God said to do. Aunt Thelma warned me of the obstacles but told me to go forward. "When God calls you to [God's] work, even if "men" say no, you can't say no to God." Each from the particularities of her faith journey helped me understand the peaks and valleys of ministry and the ensuing acceptance and rejection of my call to ministry by people of faith.

I travel out of town about three times per month. The hardest part of travel is not the waiting at the airport but taking my stuff and putting it in a piece of luggage. This seems to signify packing up pieces of myself to be displayed in an unfamiliar place in front of people who do not know me and whom I may never see again. Travel seems to be the most vulnerable aspect of the journey. As soon as I return home I immediately unpack, no matter how tired I am, so my sense of safety and security can return.

It is in those travel times that I literally revisit my journey and appreciate how far God has brought me. As I review some of the highs and lows of my own call story I realize how much they mirror those of my students and reverend sisters. Walking down memory lane, unearthing my past, and crawling back over the shards of broken glass of my life is both encumbering and cathartic. I try not to confess my stuff to any but a small group of trusted folk. It becomes so disappointing to people who think that ministers have no problems to be inundated with "fifty reasons why I hate ministry" every time women in ministry open their mouths. I avoid whiny women at all costs. It becomes so labor intensive. When my students and reverend girlfriends ask me to write my autobiography or some spiritual narrative, some memoir, I am both flattered and humbled. I am also hesitant. For I have no magic, no smoke, no mirrors, only a faith journey similar to that of other women and men who have given this sister a little help.

I remember around the time I answered my call my senior pastor saying that women ministers are thought of as either whores or lesbians. The only female ministers I had heard were single, somber, older, mad, shouted a lot, always quoted scripture, and wore black all the time. I did not know why God chose me, because I was an introvert. I was generally happy to be alive. I did not like mess. I loved men. I had a daughter. I loved to dress colorfully. I was vocally understated unless I was singing or teaching. Although I had female friends who were lesbian and some who had at one time or another stated they felt like prostitutes, I did not know how I fit either category. I came to realize that, because my speaking voice was in the alto range, I was characterized by some men as having a bedroom voice. Because I was taught to look people in the face when they are speaking and I have large eyes, I was told that I make seductive glances at men. Some assumed that because I was a women in a man's place, I was part of the so-called "master's meat," a rather disgusting practice of being the harem for visiting preachers, and that they could touch me whenever and wherever they chose. After a few preconversion conversations and calling of reinforcements from higher-ups, the practice ceased. There were assumptions that I was the one who would make the coffee for all meetings. I do not drink coffee, so I simply sat when the subject arose. I knew how to cook but did not want to support the pantry mentality that that was all I could do.

Women did not welcome me with open arms either. Some told me that I really just wanted to get close to the pastor so I could be the so-called first lady—meaning a woman raised to access church leadership through sexual relationships with or marriage to the pastor or a minister on his way up. One sister told me following my divorce that my daughter would be pregnant and on the street before she was sixteen because I could not be both a good mother *and* a good minister. There were older women in the church who would walk out or turn their chairs whenever I stood to read a scripture or say a prayer. One would wait until I began to preach to make a noisy exit. Another would call the senior pastor whenever she saw me wearing jeans or sweats. It did not seem to matter that I was working, shopping, or exercising. There were younger women and even some of my peers who said that I could never be their pastor because I was not a man. Their response was, "I am not a lesbian. A woman cannot take the place of a husband and father of their children." I have since come to term this *sexual surrogacy* in the church. There are women who construct a pseudo family with the (male) pastor as the head of their church and filler of voids in their household. Ironically, these were women who worked with me before I entered ministry.

I know that others have encountered similar situations and yet are still walking, running, crawling, and jogging through ministry. Some have turned back. Still others have refused to hear the comments or acknowledge the looks. Regardless of one's education or ordination status, there will be times in ministry when things just do not make sense. I worked on the ministerial staff of a church in Denver for about eleven years before I moved to Georgia to begin teaching at the Candler School of Theology. For the first time in my life I did not know any of the people in the churches. My daughter and I felt like aliens and visited several churches recommended by my former pastor. Finally we found a home in a small church in Lithonia. The senior pastor held two earned doctor of philosophy degrees and did not seem threatened by anyone. Having a few chapters of my own dissertation to finish while I began a new job, I was certain I had found the perfect place to do ministry. After I had worked as an associate for two years, the church split. Part of the membership moved into a new location and healing began. Then the pastor was replaced. The new pastor invited me to become the assistant pastor. I was already working with Christian education, women's ministry, young people, and the music department. I relished the opportunity and challenge of being in a new position. The first few months were wonderful. The church was growing. The music was outstanding.

There were five other wonderful reverend sisters—Kim, Rosalyn, Marie, Rosetta, and Darlene—on the ten-member ministerial staff. Yes, the senior pastor had a little different theology than I, but he seemed like a decent person. His family and my family ate dinner together occasionally. My daughter babysat his children. He even helped us move to a new house. One Watch Night Service he announced that it was time for the men in the church to take their rightful place at the head of their families and the church. The theme for the New Year would be about this movement. He asked for all the men to come to the altar. I was the only female minister in the pulpit that night and I was left alone on the platform. He called for all of the men to go get their wives and children and lead them to the altar. My husband and daughter were sitting in the congregation. I felt something in me begin to crack. I was in pain and I walked out of the sanctuary. My family and several others with whom I had worked followed me into the hall. Some of the men apologized for the pastor and said that they affirmed the ministry of all the women in the church. I understood in that moment what it might have felt like when Richard and Sarah Allen and the others left St. George's Methodist Episcopal Church in 1897 when they were prohibited from praying with White parishioners because they were freed Blacks. My husband, daughter, and I left the church and welcomed the New Year at home on our knees praying for deliverance for the church.

I knew that things were going to get even uglier after that, and they did. I was uninvited to meetings. My work was never good enough. The senior pastor began to place other persons over areas of my responsibility without telling me. Messages were transmitted to me through his stewards or officers. I would arrive for a meeting and find either the pastor or his wife in my place. I had organized and worked with the women's ministry for three years and suddenly he was expressing that I was too liberal in my teaching. (Compared to him, that was correct.) He asked the women on the staff to stop talking with the congregation during the passing of the peace. Those "sinful" women who were trying to "be men" he identified in every sermon illustration as the cause of the downfall of the family. He bragged about his managing his household like the real man that his father had taught him to be. He would drop pointed hints in the midst of his exhortations that women did not belong in ministry, that they talked too much, that they needed to leave the church, that he was the senior pastor and that was who men were supposed to be.

I had been taught by my father in ministry to be a good, supportive staff person. I learned not to discuss the habits of another elder with anyone. I learned when to speak up and when to be quiet. I recognized the authority of the office of pastor. I understood that I was not the pastor. I had no aspirations to take over anything or anybody. I just wanted a "vine and fig tree" under which to worship and serve God. I tried to be a humble, responsible servant. It is hard to be civil when one is being emotionally, spiritually, and socially abused. Another important lesson my father in ministry taught me was that being a minister did not mean being a doormat for anyone.

One by one the women on the ministerial staff began to leave the church. Two moved to New York. One just stopped coming to church. I tried to stay on but became more and more of an outcast. I began to dread going to church. I loved the congregation and had been a part of it for almost six years, but it was no longer my home. I knew that God had directed me there when I first moved to Georgia, but I had to pray that God and not my ego was keeping me there. At the same time that I was encountering hell at church, my students at Candler noticed that I was walking with a slight limp and that I had lost my smile. A group of them arranged for a massage, lunch, and driver for a Saturday afternoon of relaxation. I was thrilled. I felt so good that even going to church the next day was going to be a breeze.

I got up on Sunday morning singing. It was Youth Day. My daughter would be directing the choir. The young people with whom I had worked would be bringing the message. I felt good. I did not have to sit in the pulpit or hear negatives about women. I believed I could make it. I prayed. I sang. I danced. I rejoiced in God.

Then it was time for expressions from the pastor. I felt my body stiffen up. I thought I was losing my mind. Why was I so miserable in the house of God? I felt like screaming. How can someone else critique the message I received? I was not on a speaker phone. My call to ministry had not been transmitted on a party line, chat room, or computer network. I needed to curse. I wanted to cry. Still I had enough spiritual strength to remember that others had come to worship not to watch me collapse, act out, or diplomatically hold a come-to-Jesus meeting with the senior pastor before God and everybody. I knew that we had both answered the call to ministry. The difference was our office or assignments at that time. According to the ordination process and the laws of the denomination, we had the same rights and privileges as ordained itinerant elders.

By the time we left the church I could barely walk—his very presence made me ill. Yet I also knew that my survival skills were kicking in. My fight or flight mechanism was in full swing. I went home and rested and prayed. Monday I received a call from a steward saying that the church could no longer pay my salary but I could work if I wanted to. On Tuesday I wrote a letter to my bishop, the presiding elder, the pastor, the officers, and the ministerial staff stating my rationale for resigning from the church. I knew I would miss the people but I had to leave. I did not believe God called me to have someone constantly critiquing my call or the way I did ministry.

For the first time in my life I did not have a church home. Yet I did still have a call. I knew that God had gifted me to share the faith with others. Although I was constantly being asked to start a church, I affirmed that my call was to teach, preach, and write. It was God who had called me, not humans. Humans had told me my entire life what I could and could not do based on my race, gender, age, or their personal agendas. Through trial and error, success and failure I learned to ignore prejudicial advice and threats and listen to my spiritual source. I knew in my heart that God would provide other opportunities to do ministry. I ended up holding Wednesday evening Bible study in my dining room for about six months with others who had become disaffected with the church. I did not proselytize or encourage them to leave their churches. It took about two months to locate a new church home where I could worship freely, where my abilities were appreciated, and where I was not viewed as a threat to the senior pastor. In the interim, God opened the way for me to preach in different settings and to continue to write. The time away from an institutionalized church taught me that I wasn't really out of my head. I had been trying to function on mental, physical, social, emotional, and spiritual overload and needed to decompress in a safe space.

In my musings about ministry I ask myself the same questions I ask my students: Who called you? To whom do you answer? Who gives someone the authority to say whether or not you are telling the truth? Who saved you? What is the source of your authority? How do you define ministry? What has God done for you? What have you done for God lately? Why do you need a committee report on the validity of the issue? What is the scope of your call?

The end of the matter is this: no one knows the exact time, intent, or content of a call but God and the person God is directing toward the call. Admittedly, each of us needs a little help in our discernment process.

MOTHER WIT AND SISTAH SENSE

Reverend sister girlfriend, listen to what they never tell you in seminary or the church. Listen to these Mother Wit and Sistah Sense truisms, musings, and lessons on the call to ministry:

1. Answering a call means a close working relationship with God, not an opening to become a god.
2. Answering a call to ministry ensures both wilderness experiences and feast days.
3. No two calls are exactly alike. Some seem like precipitous labor, others like perpetual pregnancies.
4. Ministers are not messiahs, just peculiar field agents.
5. Ministers are not called because they cannot succeed at anything else.
6. Ministers are called to a higher standard of integrity.
7. Women are not called into ministry to be doormats, indentured servants, mules of the world, backbones of the church, or the glue that keeps everything and everybody else together.
8. Women are not called to become men. We are called as women to articulate faith for and from a woman's perspective.
9. Women in ministry are not called to be sexual companions or things for men in ministry.
10. Women are not called solely to work with women or children.

11. Women are not called to float above the water or to sit silently behind anyone else, but to stand boldly and firmly on holy ground as interpreters and spokeswomen for God.

12. We are not called to act as if we are better than, holier than, smarter than, or more saved than anyone else.

13. We are not called to be experts in everything.

14. We are not called to a stage but a pulpit.

15. We are not called to be the only ones in the family, church, school, or community to pray or preach.

16. We are not called to pimp the people or prostitute ourselves.

17. We are not called to like everyone but we are expected to love everyone.

18. We are not called to be asexual. Our children are not conceived by immaculate conception.

19. We are not called to twenty-four-hour, three-hundred-and-sixty-five-day, seven-day-a-week, twelve-month, no sabbatical, no rest, no-time-for-rest ministries. Jesus modeled healthy time off.

20. We can go to the party as long as we do not become the party.

21. We are not called with enhanced photographic memory for everyone's name, face, or personal business.

22. Answering a call to ministry does not change the sexual preference of our spouse or partner.

23. Answering a call to ministry does not mean our children will be dysfunctional "preacher's kids," specially gifted, or next in line to answer a call.

24. Answering a call to ministry does not ensure great singing voices, no bad hair days, no weight gain, or no runs in our pantyhose.

25. Answering the call does not make one a theological encyclopedia, preaching machine, or penultimate healer.

26. There will be times when even your closest friends will not believe you are called.

27. If you answered the call merely for fame, fortune, power, or prestige, you picked up the wrong message. Run now!!!

28. Strength for this journey does not come by osmosis. Ministry is hard work and takes place not just on Sunday morning.

29. If God called you to preach, then preach, but if God called you to teach, write, sing, administer, nurture, pastor, or visit the sick, then do that, and let no one tell you anything different.

30. Doubt of the call does not make you a bad person. It makes you more prayerful and appreciative of the opportunity.

These lessons are by no means all I have learned or that has been taught by my mentors. They are only musings of the moment. After all this time I still need to hear that still small voice telling me that I am called by God to do God's ministry in God's way under God's protective direction. At times a mournful spiritual refrain like "They treat me so mean here, Lord, I wish I never was born. Lord, how come me here?" puts me into my "God, I-know-you-did-not-mean-me" mode. In other instances the powerful encouragement of the spiritual lyrics "Ride on, King Jesus, no (man) can a hinder me," gives me more strength than I ever imaged as I pursue my call.

In 1999 I was to present workshops on women preachers for the Connectional African Methodist Episcopal Women in Ministry (A.M.E./WIM), held in St. Louis, Missouri, during a snowstorm. Several registered presenters and attendees were unable to attend due to the weather and conflicts in other church matters. I was holding the WIM consultant office of Personal and Interpersonal Development. The A.M.E./WIM president at that time, Rev. Sandra E. H. Smith Blair, was a personal reverend sisterfriend, so I did whatever she asked me to do. Rev. Sandra commandeered me to substitute for someone by assigning me the task of saying a few words to the women during the Saturday morning prayer breakfast. I was to encourage my reverend sisters to keep on helping each other as they walked the path of ministry. I struggled most of the night, and early that Saturday morning God gave me "A Letter from Jarena Lee." I cried as I wrote verbatim what I heard God place in my spirit as the voice of Jarena Lee, the female preaching icon for the denomination. I tried to imagine what she would say to us twentieth-century women preachers in order to mentor us. This is an excerpt of the self-published (in the rich tradition of my preaching foremothers) minisermon I gave that day:

Dear Daughters,
I want you to know, my sisters, you have to be persistent. When they turn you away, keep going back, and going back, and going back, and going back, and going back . . .

When God calls you, when God anoints you, when God appoints you, when God puts words in your mouth and sets you before the people, know that you have been set aside, sanctified, and ordained by God to do God's work. No need for human conversation, criticism, or committee. God said it and that settles it. God's calling is a foundation of our ordination. No one can deny us what God has for us. Nothing and nobody can stop the move of God . . .

My sisters, please note that every time you pray—I'm ordained.

Every time you send a song—I'm ordained.

Every time you have a word of testimony—I'm ordained.

Every time you bring a word of hope even when they make you stand outside the door—I'm ordained.

Every time you take a stand for justice— I'm ordained.

Every time you give a cup of cold water in Jesus' name— I'm ordained.

Every time you refuse to give up on your call—I'm ordained.

Every time you take the assignment in that little church they said was about to die and God blesses the effort and it thrives—I'm ordained.

Every time, every time, every time you yield to God's indwelling spirit instead of outside influences—I'm ordained . . .

Your lives today, my daughters, help affirm for me that God is still calling, ordaining, and blessing women with all kinds of gifts and graces. So just keep on, daughters.

Keep on praying . . . and preaching . . . and teaching . . . and living . . . and loving . . . and ministering . . . and giving your lives to Christ.

The Bible says that what we obtain is not by power or by might but by God's Spirit.

Keep in mind that every tear you shed on the journey, every pain you feel on the journey, every lonely night you spend on the journey, every headache you experience on the journey, every joy you share on the journey, every victory you have on the journey is all to the glory of God.[1]

Well, that's the best I can do for now. I will keep you on my prayer list as you continue your journey. If you want to talk further the best way to reach me is via e-mail.

Love,
Dr. T

---

1. See Fry Brown, *Weary Throats and New Songs*, 46–52, for the entire sermon.

TWO

⬚

E X P R E S S
Y O U R S E L F

⬚

Hey Sis,

I know we are supposed to be quiet about this, but I just can't keep this inside. Are you on another line? I can call back later if you need me to. Okay, I'll hold for a bit while you finish that call. No, it's not exactly life and death, but it could be. Look here, I was just thinking about how we can help Lynn speak up when those people ignore her. Child, you know she knows how to talk. She's not stupid or anything. I talk with her about once a week. She's just afraid she'll say the wrong thing. How will they know who she is if she never opens her mouth?

The folk saying from Ghana, "Until the Lion has his (her) own storyteller, the hunter will always have the best part of the story,"[1] is echoed repeatedly in the lives of Black women. No one can adequately tell our stories but us. Truth lies in the ex-

---

1. Ewe-mina (Benin, Ghana, and Togo) proverb, folk saying.

perience and the willingness to pass on information from a particular social location. In an age of female televangelists, webcasts, iPods, and conference preachers, one might assume there are no barriers left for women in ministry. Surely, if one believes the advertisements for the next big women's conference or watches cable television's religious programming with clergy couples, soloists, and "faithful women" talk shows, one might think history has righted itself and ecclesiastical apartheid has been abolished.

The reality is that while there have certainly been some gains in the past twenty-five years, with election of female bishops or a handful of millionaire women preachers, there are denominations that deny, rescind, or ghettoize women's ordination. In some cases women are ordained but are not granted opportunities to pastor. Women who "rock the boat" or try to voice their disdain for the rules and regulations are characterized as castrating, promiscuous, incorrigible, destructive, and confused about their sexuality. Sociohistorically the rap has been that women seeking to enter ministry are not real women—that their actions will destroy the family system. That their voices are too weak to "say a word." That they will take jobs God meant for men. That men will stop attending church because there will be too many women in leadership. That it's just unnatural for women to handle holy things, or that only women will listen to them. And the beat goes on . . .

I attended seminary in Denver, Colorado, and eventually was the only Black woman in my doctoral program. At the beginning of my program I was working on the staff of Shorter African Methodist Episcopal Church and was trying to navigate on several levels what it means to be a woman in ministry. In the church I was directed to Jarena Lee as a role model (along with reminders that she was never ordained) as if no other Black women ever entered ministry. I knew that I would not walk twenty-five hundred miles in one year, leave my child with others, or preach on street corners. But I knew that I could handle

myself in public. After all, I had been taught to fight off offend-
ers, both verbally and physically. I was raised as the second oldest of seven children and grew up with boys as playmates, so I
knew little fear. But this ministry thing scared the hell out of me.

The other women in my denomination who were striving to
be leaders were hundreds of miles away, so supportive conversations were out of the question. I would see them perhaps once a
year at a conference. The male ministers denigrated most of them
as "dragon ladies," "angry bitches," "man haters," "want–to–be's,"
"poor excuses for mother," "too ugly to find a man," and "bishop's
prostitutes." Conformity was and is the rule of the day in church
life. The resounding message was that if one wished to survive the
system, the chief operating vocabulary was one of compliance,
acquiescence, assimilation, allegiance, conventionality, submission, or willingness to be like others.

I heard the jokes about women as I entered the office for
preservice prayers, in the pulpit as women walked down aisles,
and in the parking lot following service. There were congregants who felt led to make it their life's work to issue some
"helpful" proclamation each time they saw me. You have heard
them yourself, I'm sure. "No respectable woman would be in
there with all those men." "Are you a lesbian or something?
That's what I heard about all you women preachers." "Girl,
don't you want to get married again and have a couple of children?" "You stepping awfully high but you are not better than
we are." "You just need to get laid. Then you'd be a woman
again." "You'll get tired pretty soon." I rarely heard anything
positive about women in ministry, even from women, although
these were some of the same people who voted to issue me a license to preach.

I was angry with God and disgusted with people. All I wanted
to do was teach. I did not want to be the pastor. I certainly did not
want to be a man. I was not going to sleep my way to the top, either. I tried to go on autopilot at church and invest my energy in
school. I seemed to be stuck in the midst of an identity crisis. I

was anxious, conflicted, and confused.[2] I was stressed trying to determine who I was and how I was going to survive. I was an introvert by nature and had a history of struggling to find and use my voice. I prayed for guidance, but it seemed like every time God gave me a "go ahead and do what I said," some human being would try to derail me. That was part of my confusion in God calling me. I was perfectly happy singing, reading, and teaching small groups. At work there was always this cognitive dissonance—saying one thing and doing another, can't quite connect all the dots, trying to move through the confusion, know that this is not the first time nor will it be the last these events occur. I was trying to do the will of God but it seemed like I was on the losing team.

Even at my seminary, I was confronted with finding where I fit. It seemed that all the people of faith were located in a history of great white men, crusading white women, and exceptional Black men. Whenever I pushed the envelope and asked about Black women I was met with conciliatory conversations driven by the need to placate me. I would hear people say things like, "Don't get me wrong, but. . . ." There was lack of eye contact and almost an apology for Black women not being important or an inability to locate books about Black women. With no mentors I felt betrayed by God for making me enter ministry; I felt as if I had no choice but to do what God said, and yet I felt abandoned. I was desperate for someone who looked, sounded, and acted like me and who had experienced what I had lived.

It was my history of religion professor, Jean Miller Schmidt, who opened the door to my future by introducing me to Anna Julia Cooper. Cooper was a nineteenth-century educator, a member of the so-called Talented Tenth, and an international human rights activist. She lived an arduous and faith-filled life

---

2. A psychosocial state or condition of disorientation and role confusion occurring as a result of conflicting internal and external experiences, pressures, and expectations and often producing acute anxiety. *The American Heritage® Dictionary of the English Language*, 4th ed. (New York: Houghton Mifflin Company, 2000, 2003).

from 1858 to 1964. Dr. Cooper worked untiringly for women's liberation. She organized schools and clubs to forward the cause of women's equality within society in general and the Black community and church in particular. I recommend her life story to women whenever I have the chance, particularly for women who are over forty, those contemplating a change in vocation, or those who feel stalled in their life situation. In 1892 Cooper convincingly argued in *A Voice from the South by a Colored Woman from the South*, "Only the BLACK WOMAN can say 'when and where I enter,' in the quiet, undisputed dignity of my womanhood, without violence and without suing or special patronage, then and there the whole . . . race enters with me."[3]

It is a passage I interpret as being about engaging power disparities and voicing my opinion without fear of reprisal. Cooper's words revived in me the survival instructions that had been modeled, verbalized, and even physically instilled in me by the women in my family, neighborhood, and church: I could challenge without cursing. I could address a situation without hatred regardless of how much I was hurting. I could express myself without losing my womanhood. Cooper believed that women should speak for themselves, write, and live their own history.

> It is not the intelligent woman vs. the ignorant woman; nor the white woman vs. the black, the brown and the red—it is not even the cause of woman vs. man. Nay I say, 'tis woman's strongest vindication for speaking that *the world needs to hear her voice*. It would be subversive of every human interest that the cry of one-half the human family be stifled.[4]

Her italicized words became a mantra for me: "People need to hear MY voice! MY voice is just as important as anyone else's.

---

3. Anna Julia Cooper, *A Voice from the South by a Colored Woman from the South* (Xenia, Ohio: Aldine Press, 1892, New York: Oxford University Press, 1988), 31.
4. Ibid., 121.

The church and the academy must hear from Teresa Lynn Fry in order for things to change. I need to hear MY own voice." When my ideas were rejected or someone "piggybacked" or "dovetailed" on something I said and received credit, I learned to rephrase it and remind the men that I had said the same thing. I learned never to give all my ideas or information. People have a tendency to steal even work in progress. I learned to speak up even when no one seemed to be listening. I challenged myself to speak out with well-honed and researched excellence. Engraved in my mind were my mother's words, "Don't act like you don't know. If you don't know or don't remember, go look it up!" I decided I would no longer let the hunter speak for me. I wanted to be able to tell not only the best part but the truest part. Over time I have learned that conformity can be seductive, disingenuous, tempting, or alluring. It may mean the path of least resistance, but that route has never been an option for a Black woman born in America. Dr. Cooper's book, coupled with the voices of my elders, became the portal to my deconstruction and reconstruction of the history of Black women and a means for undergirding how I expressed my femininity and faith.

The 1970s were replete with songs about being roaring women, natural women, invincible women, and surviving women. I loved the songs and occasionally played them for hours to shore up my courage for engaging the world and to celebrate my gender power. During my early activist days I read Michelle Wallace's 1978 classic *Black Macho and the Myth of the Super Woman* from cover to cover about ten times. It is an in-depth political analysis of the status of Black women and their predilection for trying to be super strong, able to endure all things, and deny self to the point of death.[5] On this side of

---

5. See Michele Wallace, "Variations on Negation and the Heresy of Black Feminist Creativity," in *Reading Black, Reading Feminist*, ed. Henry Louis Gates Jr. (New York: Meridian, 1990), 52–67, for a brief overview of her analysis.

thirty I realize that these sung and written opinions were the continuation of the centuries' old task of women expressing their right to been seen and heard. They were also a means of using language to encourage women to think of themselves as fully human. These songs were like a rebirth, helping to take off demeaning images of women and put on divine designer "I am somebody" labels.

Language is one of the most powerful tools women in ministry have at their disposal. Language expresses one's heart, soul, and mind. Language is socially shaped through traditional or contemporary values and usage. It is informational and dialogical. Language is culturally specific. Language assists us in unearthing the depth of our spirituality and emotion. Language stems the "everybody is doing it" mentality with a "because God said do it" thought process. Revisiting the language of the church that says that everything is male is a first step. No, I do not advocate throwing out God as Father. That image was critical for me growing up and having a tentative relationship with my birth father. I needed a father figure who would see me as a special person and protect me from any danger. God the Father was that person.

I remember receiving my seminary theology paper with a big red "F" at the top and bloody marks throughout the body of the text. The only "F" I had ever received in my life was on a genetics paper in college. I was on scholarship. What was wrong with the professor? I knew I had studied the material and had a good grasp of the information. I made an appointment with my professor, who, it felt to me, proceeded to tear me apart for my sexist view of God. I was stunned. She then ran through inclusive language guidelines but, more important, why using language to include all persons was imperative. Exclusionary language denies full personhood to women, children, elders, homosexuals, the poor, the homeless, or the disabled in particular and others in general. I sat for a minute and explained why I used what I now understand was exclusive language. She waited a minute and then said, "I understand, but in my class use inclusive language or you will fail this class and all the others in seminary." Thankfully, I was allowed to rewrite the paper.

After more research and social analysis of the use of God talk to oppress and exclude people, primarily women and the disabled, I began to understand a new concept for speaking about God. I was captivated by the realization that I was made in the image of God. God was multifaceted like a diamond. I was created as a particular facet of a larger creation. God through me was a Black, divorced, full figured, gray haired, college educated, itinerant preaching woman who happened to be a single mother. God became everything and everyone around me. I came to believe in a God who created all persons as equals. Why would that same God think less of women?

Since that day in 1985, I have used inclusive and now balanced language. I think through who is listening, whom I am leaving out, whom I am offending, whom I am hurting, and who God is to me at that time. I believe that God is both male and female. I do not refer to God as he/she or some other androgynous language. I try to use a variety of gender neutral language depending on the context. There are times I say Father God, other times Mother God, sometimes God who helps me write this book or God who is preaching this sermon. I use inclusive language in all my publications and sermons. Inclusive language or balanced language in terms of the age, the culture, the gender, the background of my audience is a given. When teaching about balanced language in classes, Bible studies, and seminars, I make sure I say why it is important. That way, I hope those I teach understand that I am not someone who hates the God of my ancestors but rather one who tries to be "no respecter of persons." The exception is seminary classes where there is a written requirement to use inclusive language. I try not to rip the spiritual foundation out of the household of faith without telling the occupants why they need a linguistic renovation. It is through language that women in ministry can rename themselves children of God, daughters of the covenant, and hand-made, God-breathed humanity. It is through voice that they inform the world of who they are.

As a former speech pathologist, I am keenly aware of voices. Voice demonstrates one's ability to communicate a message clearly and effectively. The listener attends to the voice and determines what the speaker feels, intends, knows, or perceives. Small wonder that when a speaker has been repeatedly told her opinion does not matter, she is likely to begin to keep it to herself. Sticks and stones may not break bones, but I do believe they can kill one's spirit. Name calling oftentimes hurts more than physical hits because one can recall the names long after the bruises have healed. In like manner, when a woman is told day after day that her opinion does not matter or her needs are of no consequence, something happens to her spirit, and the toxicity of the pain begins to corrode her vocal cords.

I have a reverend sister friend who is absolutely brilliant. She is a master of language. She passionately loves God. Yes, she has her idiosyncrasies, but who doesn't? I witnessed her go through silence to expression and back again. When I first met this sister she was working as an associate minister at a growing church. She had been a senior pastor but relinquished that position due to family concerns. She sacrificially worked above and beyond the required ministry because she loved God and God's people. Having myself done the same type of job in another city, I understood her passion to ensure that the church ran smoothly. She juggled several positions and filled in for those who were unable to complete their tasks.

Yet I avoided her the first few weeks because she seemed so sad, like sisters look just before they either snap or disintegrate. I was in the midst of a healing process from another church war and just did not have the energy to help out another sister. Sometimes you give out so much of yourself that before you know it you are running on empty and you cannot find your self any more.

It so happened that right around that time one of my younger blood sisters visited and told me that I needed to make friends with this very reverend sister and give her as much help, assistance, support, and sistership as I could. I asked why, for it seemed obvious to me that she did not want my help. My sister said I should do it "because that is what you do." I vowed to try as soon as I got it together.

A few weeks later I introduced myself and asked if she needed to talk. I discovered that this sister had also come through a church battle from which her scars were so deep that she was going through a healing process herself. She had been bruised so deeply that she chose not to talk with anyone but God. She was quiet until she prayed or preached. We began to encourage each other into not only speaking but tending to our self-care. During the next two years we watched each other's backs, bandaged each other's wounds, helped each other's families, and shared sister secrets. Then the muffling effects of church life began again.

Churches are like demilitarized zones. They are quiet until someone decides to put on a show of strength or they are bored with peace and launch an ungodly rocket into the midst of praying people. As casualties mount it seems that people forget that faith they talked about before the war began. It felt like someone was sitting on our chests and our voices were becoming compromised. I watched this reverend sister slip back into her old habits of doubting her skills, second-guessing her beliefs, and vocalizing everything with an exasperated heaviness. It took all my "sister needs me" strength to try to keep her engaged until other family matters began to sap my energy. She soon reverted to her previous brooding, discouraged, heartbreaking, and silent state. She refused to return calls or e-mails and asked that we not drop by her house as had been our habit. She occasionally sent a text message to let me know she was alive but there was no face-to-face contact.

About a month later, I called her cell phone to check in before I left the country and was greeted with her cheerful voice.

She said that she was fine and had just needed some singular healing time. She had to get rid of some stuff and reclaim her life away from church and support systems. She had battled internal and external foes and had come out as the person she had suppressed for five years. She was almost giddy. Instead of smothering death there was new life in her voice. She told me not to worry. She still had some work to do. She intended never to let the pressures of other ministers or church systems suppress her voice and creativity again. I was fine with that. She was breathing and happy. Sometimes the best way to help out a sister is to leave her alone for a while.

And sometimes it is you who has to get away by yourself. Sometimes it is you who has to find some distance from all the stuff that is sapping your vocal energy. Sometimes the voice telling you so emerges in a whisper and sometimes it floods the room. Whatever the volume, get the stuff out of your system, out of your space, out of your head, and off your shoulders. Let it go. Release it. Once that external pressure is gone, talk to yourself until your own voice grows stronger. You may need to begin by whispering until you rediscover yourself if you can't hear your voice initially. You can even use sign language until you recover sufficiently spiritually to leave the wilderness and find your voice again.

And when you do, when you find your voice again, hold on to it and do not be dissuaded from its tones. Women preachers are sometimes criticized for not sounding "like preachers," meaning they do not have deep, resonant, fiery, captivating, and powerful voices as some imagine God's voice to be. While there are indeed women with commanding voices, society stereotypically characterizes women's voices as being seductive, playful, pleasant, sensual, comforting, nurturing, whiney, shrill, or angry. Critiquing a woman's voice as a means to discount her ministerial call is pathetic at best. Aren't there plenty of male preachers whose voices aren't fiery and powerful? My women students enter preaching classes with distinctive voice issues.

They are muted and silenced, loud and angry, harsh and hesitant, authoritative and moderate, brusque and accusing, mellow and seasoned, and fatigued and searching. Regardless of the volume, pitch, or fluency, each voice tells something about the women's personality, experience, vocal role models, and comfort level in the preaching moment.

Major difficulty arises when a woman is unable to speak up, is apologetic, or believes that by imitating male vocal delivery she will be accepted as a preacher. This assessment is exacerbated among Black preaching due to the prominence of "hooping,"[6] or vocal celebration at the close of a sermon. In some circles if the one preaching does not employ physical or vocal gymnastics—repetition, hesitancy, scale running, pregnant pauses, shouting, singing, or sweating profusely—then that person is called a speaker rather than a preacher. In order to avoid such classification, women have adapted to male delivery modes or turned to a guttural sounding delivery. They may do irreparable damage by straining their smaller (not weaker!) vocal mechanisms.

To make the point, I sometimes ask my students to play a tape, CD, or DVD of how Jesus or Paul sounded when they preached! I must have missed the text about "Jesus hooped." Certainly, I hoop from time to time but I have never practiced a hoop. I believe that when one is directed by God to a place beyond one's control, one sometimes says something one did not intend and in a manner that surprises one. However, I also believe that God instructs us to use our voices with integrity and common sense. Everyone has a distinct communicative style. Some speakers are direct and "in your face," others are subtle and indirect, and still others depend on others to talk for them. Identify the style that works for you. It may differ according to the situation, but try to speak as yourself and for yourself.

---

6. For a fuller explanation of "hooping," see Teresa Fry Brown, *Weary Throats and New Songs: Black Women Proclaiming* (Nashville: Abingdon Press, 2003), 166–75.

Such being one's true self extends also to how one dresses. When I began my ministerial journey, women had few options for clerical attire. Acceptable ministerial dress for women seemed to be based on that of nineteenth-century evangelists. It was as if the ordination coordinators held up the well-circulated picture of Jarena Lee wearing long black fitted dresses, black laced-up boots, huge bonnets, no makeup, hair pulled back, and long sleeves and gloves, and decided that all women should dress like her. It did not seem to matter that men meanwhile were wearing a rainbow array of suits or robes with color-coordinated shoes, bright ties, and multiple rings. One such man explained to me that in nature the male species always is more colorful than the female. I understood that that was probably true but opined that I am not a bird. My cynical self chalked such behavior up to some men overcompensating. Robes were made of yards of black fabric that overwhelmed women's often more petite frames. Some women were fortunate enough to sew or find women who designed robes just for women. Collared shirts lacked darts and allowance for full breasts. The alternative dress was a black or navy blue suit with a long skirt and white blouse. Some women wore suits tailored by men to be more acceptable to the congregation. Clothing "speaks" louder than words at times.

When I told my paternal grandmother, Grandma Cloria, that I was entering ministry the first thing she said was, "Granny" (she said I had an old soul so that was her nickname for me), "if I ever see you or think that you are dressing or looking a like a man, I will get up out of my grave and whip your butt! God made you a woman so dress and act like one. Don't be like that woman we have at the church." Grandma Cloria never made idle threats. Ironically she died the next year and three years later at my paternal grandfather's funeral "that" woman was in the pulpit.

She exemplified everything my board of examiners wanted me to do. She wore black from head to toe. She had close-cropped hair gelled back in a rather masculine style. She wore no jewelry, no makeup, and black, thick-soled shoes. She spoke with a booming baritone voice. Her movement across the pulpit was plodding, with her shoulders thrust forward. I knew I was in trouble when, in the middle of my Grandma Cloria's funeral, my maternal grandmother Mama Tessie leaned over and said, with reference to "that" woman preacher: "Teresa Lynn Fry, that's why women have such a hard time in ministry. See how she's dressed. She has been the talk of the town ever since she came here. She looks like she wears her husband's clothes. You wear your own things." I believe in the wisdom of my elders. I also believed that my grandmothers would never tell me something that would not help me.

I have lived my entire ministry literally skirting the edge of male-established decorum. I have enough sense to know that if black is required because of the occasion such as an ordination or other special ceremony, I can wear color as an accent or undergarments. I have owned one clergy collar in my life. I wore a collar twice the first year after my diaconal ordination. I was visiting members in hospitals and at the time people were more likely to accept women as "real" ministers if they wore collars or habits. I found the shirt so uncomfortable and for me so inappropriate that I packed it away. While I understand why women wear them (besides denominational requirements), I found my ministerial authority in God's direction rather than in a piece of cloth. The down side is there are costs to being myself (ostracism, gossip, punishment, and ridicule, to name a few). The upside is I recognize myself when I look in the mirror. I am not a carbon copy of someone else, nor a piece of the scenery.

Now sisters, don't get it twisted. I am not trying to stand out from the crowd, just stand up for who I am. I do not defy authorities because I have nothing better to do with my time. There have been many days when I thought, "Why don't I just show up butt naked and then they will be happy. God did not include a dress code in my call. This is too much of a hassle."

Discussions of dress or appearance for women ministers are like viewing marathon showings of the popular cable shows *What Not to Wear* or *America's Top Model*. An inordinate amount of time is spent discussing color pallets, skirt lengths, jewelry, shoe heights, robe styles, hairstyles, and accessories. I can't believe the hype. With the possible exception of those male preachers who have decided that their pectorals and biceps must be exposed to attract more female members, those whose suit collections resemble a bag of Skittles, or those whose overstuffed cassock sash keeps getting lost under their lower abdomen, there are no critiques of or rules about men's ministerial attire. Robe designs are decidedly male, with openings for pants pockets even when the style is cut down for women. Attire for women ministers ranges from fur and sequin encrusted after-five wear to designer knit suits, to tailored pantsuits to brocade cassocks, to Seven jeans and tee shirts. In some circles, the more flamboyant the dress the more clout the woman is thought to have. Some sisters elect themselves as fashion barometers or permission givers for other women. Usually there is a small group of women, called "the circuit" because they exchange appearances at each other's conferences, who decide to set the standard for all things "reverend sister." The Black woman preacher "success ensemble" from the late 1990s to the present is St. John knits, though I'm not sure why, because the knits do not work with every sister's body and the expense is beyond most women ministers' budgets.

Depending on the denomination, most sisters wear all white or black with no accessories or opt for deep jewel tones or Africentric prints. Faces are whipped with MAC, Prescriptives, Fashion Fair, L'Oreal HIP, Cover Girl Queen Collection, Nars, or Revlon, or kept bare with shea butter or Vaseline added for a natural shine. Jewelry over the past twenty years has moved from understated studs to huge diamond chandeliers swinging from earlobes, from no rings to a five carat diamond on each finger, and from small gold crosses to enormous backbreaking items larger than the cross of Calvary. Hair styles range from relaxed to locks with color from platinum blonde to salt and pepper gray. Some sisters opt for lapcloths and head coverings while others are appalled by those practices. I think that sisters know when their skirt is too short before they leave home regardless of how high the pulpit may be. If we do not have access to a mirror, there are enough windows along the way to check our appearance. The lacy handkerchiefs or shawls that must be readjusted constantly or removed every time one stands up are more of a distraction than "modesty" item, but to each her own.

I love shoes. I own about sixty pairs of heels of various styles and colors that are color coded and kept in clear plastic boxes in two closets in my home. I am a premium customer of Zappos.com. Some of my reverend sisters affectionately call me Imelda. When I was a little girl I had a pair of play shoes and a pair of Sunday shoes. I prayed to God that when I was grown I would go without food if God would let me have more than two pair of shoes. God is faithful and I do not miss the calories! It took another sister to tell me that I inadvertently set some style standards for women in the congregation and on the ministerial staff. My shoe selection is determined by what I wear but my outfit is covered by the robe. My femininity was being verified by my shoes and I was unaware the women commented on them each week.

While on the ministerial staff in Denver, one of the mothers of the church, Miss Carmina, would give me money quarterly to go to the beauty salon and to purchase new shoes. She told me that I represented all the women in the church and I had to come "correct." I was entreated to make sure my hair was always neat and clean. She did not care what color or style I chose (I dyed my hair deep auburn until I was thirty-eight and came to accept the gray hair as evidence of the real me) as long as it was fashionably styled. I was instructed not to buy black shoes but to buy shoes to match my clothes so when I attended meetings or events after service I would look like a young woman.

I realize that there are generational standards of dress. Miss Carmina was the age of my grandmothers but I appreciated her intention. While I was in seminary I worked and went to school full time. I also was raising my daughter and working at the church. As I have said before, the "strong Black woman" will die if something does not give.

I decided the last year of my masters program in seminary to cut off all my hair and go natural. I had worn the style prior to moving to Denver and knew that it would be a great time-saving measure. Well, one would have thought the world had come to an end the first time I went to church after that haircut. People thought I had lost my mind. A few asked why I had cut off "their beautiful hair." Talk about absurd statements. Next the questions regarding my femininity floated to the top of the critique list. I was still Teresa but they decided I did not look like a woman anymore. It did not seem to matter that there were other women in the church with closely cropped naturals. There seems to be a different set of dress codes for women in ministry.

There is a special burden of being the one or ones who represents the femininity of "all" the women of the church. When you think about it, women in ministry are up in front of the congregation and are more visible than other women. I am not saying we *are* representative of all women, just that some women think we are. I have been called a whore to my face by two women in ministry because of my dress choices. One took umbrage because I generally wore my hair relaxed and shoulder length. She had difficulty growing her hair. Her contention was that my hair was too seductive. I was her senior. I chose not to follow her advice to pull my hair back into a bun. She went on the offensive. This sister, who had been married multiple times, called me a whore in front of younger ministers. I will take a lot of things, particularly from people who do not know any better, sister. But a bishop had to catch my fist right before I decked her that day.

The other woman was an elder senior. I was sitting in the back at a district conference listening to pastors' reports because I had just come from taking a midterm exam. The presiding elder introduced the new pastor, who had been assigned to fill a long-standing vacancy where I had been a supply pastor. She was my senior chronologically and in ordination status. I did not know her but was glad a woman pastor in my denomination was now in the area. She wore a severe upswept hairstyle, a collar, and always black clothes. As I have said, my dress was not flashy but it was never bland. Her bearing was regal as she rose to take the microphone. She cleared her throat and then proceeded, in over-enunciated discourse, to address the conference. She waxed on for about fifteen minutes about her ministry, life, and how glad she was to be in the district. I was raised to respect my elders so I overlooked most of her derogatory comments about young people in ministry, why seminary was not necessary, her connection to male colleagues, or her special privilege due to her age and status. I figured she had been thorough enough stuff to break the path for me and that she was entitled to her opinions. Then she took an unexpected turn that shattered the sister connection.

She said that she noticed there were about five other women in the meeting. She then went on to say she did not know why the board of ministerial examiners would admit whorish women who wore anything but black and who wore nail polish. My head snapped up and she was pointing at me. Everything went white before me. I had fought the men for three years and now a woman was attacking my appearance. The next thing I knew, my presiding elder had me by the hand and was leading me out of the church. To this day I do not know what I said or did. The elder told me to ignore her because she did not know me, just that I apparently violated her standards of feminine appearance. In a twist of fate, the next year she got married and showed up at annual conference in a robin's egg blue suit, makeup, and heels. She never apologized for her assessment of me. I surmised that she had had no other models of women in ministry other than herself and that I presented too much internal conflict for her. It did not make the affront more palatable. I became conscious of the fact that sometimes a reverend sister's image of what is acceptable dress for women in ministry is just as confining as that of the congregation.

I was sitting in a pulpit about ten years ago prayerfully anticipating how the sermon would be received. As the worship leader introduced me I became increasingly uncomfortable. I believe in buying shoes that fit. I have worn about a three-and-a-half- to four-inch heel since I was eighteen. I am more relaxed in heels than flats. I can wear heels for fourteen hours a day. As the introduction ended my feet felt too large for my shoes. I knew that I had taken my meds and had not eaten, so my feet should not have been swollen. I did not know what to do because I had about three minutes until I was to deliver the sermon. As is my habit I knelt down to pray for guidance in the preaching moment and in my spirit God said, "Take off your shoes." I thought I misunderstood so I prayed for calm and no confusion during the sermon. Again I heard "Take off your shoes." I am usually compliant when I know I have heard from God so I took off my heels and set them under the chair. When I stood up to preach I felt more grounded and comfortable in the pulpit than ever. Early on, my father in ministry, the late Jesse Boyd, had joked about my inability to jump up and spin around when I preached because my heels might get caught in the carpet. That was not the rationale for taking off my shoes. My ordination board had told me that I needed to wear flats or one-inch chunky heels so I would not be a distraction to men when I preached. That was not the reason either. I figure men should be responsible for their own fetishes. Over the years others have asked if that day I was trying to do that whole Moses taking off his sandals thing. That was not it either. I think that all ground is holy because it was created by God. On that day as I stood barefoot in the pulpit I felt closer to God than ever. I felt that I could do anything God said. I felt vulnerable and naked, yet also powerful. I have only preached in shoes twice in the last ten years. I am termed a flatfoot preacher in that I generally stand behind the pulpit when I preach. In those times when the Spirit moves me to walk around, women comment that "I knew we were in for it when you took off your shoes." It is too difficult to explain that I do not understand fully why or when I take off my shoes; it just happens. I do try to wear pumps or mules without straps when I preach so I am not doing a distracting disrobing act in the pulpit like men taking off ties or throwing jackets on the floor.

Speaking of pulpit presence, remember when your Mama told you to always have on clean underwear? Preaching is a vigorous activity. There are times one gets caught up in the worship service and physically loses control. If you wear only a slip under your robe make sure it is long enough to cover you when you wake up with your robe unzipped because the ushers were trying to revive you. Hearing discussions about how to get you up off the floor and not show your bra rather defeats that whole "slain in the spirit" moment. Sisters who preach hard can feel that gush of sweat going down the back and front. Try to have a handkerchief in your Bible or purse. Nothing looks worse than that leftover white Kleenex sisters try to use to dab off the pool of menopausal water collecting on their necks and faces. Showers after service are not always an option, particularly between multiple services and with a dinner immediately following last service.

Carrying a change of clothing, especially underwear, along with deodorant and a wet washcloth in a baggie is a great practice for a quick hygiene check.

I recall preparing for the baptism of my niece and my former choir director. The church had a large heated pool under the pulpit area. I put on one of the staff's black baptismal robes and some nonskid socks over an old slip, black bra and black panties as instructed by the stewardesses. I was too short to wear the rubber hip boots the senior pastor wore under his robe. Although I was the first woman to enter the pool, I was assured that I was appropriately dressed. All I knew is that I was about to perform my first immersion baptism. People began to gather around the pool. Cameras were chronicling the historic occasion. The choir was praising God for the new souls. The senior pastor was reciting the baptismal liturgy. Surely, God was in this place.

As soon as I planted both feet on the bottom of the pool, the water began to envelop my legs and my robe began to rise to my waist. The more I batted it down the more it billowed with water. All I could think about was whether I had on clean underwear without holes. The holiness of the baptism became secondary for what seemed like an hour. In actuality it took about three minutes to secure the robe between my legs and extend my hand to my niece. On Monday morning I sewed about fifteen drapery weights into the hem of the robe, put my name on it and knew I would be better prepared the next time. I have kept one of the pictures of the "floating robe" to remind me to always wear good, clean underwear, especially to church.

Over the past twelve years, I have worked diligently to eradicate concerns about people and situations that seek to silence me as well as concerns about what I should wear or not wear. In my role as seminary professor, I indirectly and directly mentor women at the entry level of ministry. They range from highly educated second- or third-career women close to my age to women fresh out of undergraduate education around the age of my daughter, with little or no work experience. Regardless of their background, they routinely ask questions about expectations for presence and dress. Whether they have been known for exquisite élan or thrift store chic they worry about appropriate presentation in ministerial situations. Women who have held positions as university professors or CEOs of their own companies and young independent campus leaders evidence trepidation before a new power structure. They fear alienation and seek permission for everything they say or do.

In many cases they seem to have replaced their sense of empowerment with an institution's, group's, board's, or some person's suffocating in-powerment. I have been there and done that. When the desire to become something that you never imagined you could be becomes so overwhelming that you cannot think of anything else, you may relinquish power to someone else until a goal is attained. "In-powerment" is a word I made up to describe the dictation of ascribed characteristics, total control of a person's life, or means of using another's gifts by a person or persons who exercise power over that individual. It has been my experience over the years that women who are required to obtain permission incessantly from those "in power" for everything they say or do in ministry are in danger of becoming voiceless, discontented, petulant, and indecisive. Yes, I respect the leadership of the church or academy, but God gave me a mind also. Whether they concern my story, voice, language, attire, or mannerisms, I try not to allow decisions I make for myself to adversely affect others. I am never defiant for the sake of being defiant, but I know myself and do not enjoy the marionette experiences prevalent in ministry. To me, "empowerment" means that an individual takes back her voice, body, mind, soul, spirit, and life from external decision makers. Empowered women speak when they need to, decide what they believe, stand where they feel comfortable, wear what they choose, decide where they go, and affirm themselves instead of waiting for a committee report.

The core of self-expression is grounded in knowing who you are and remembering that God and not some human being created you. As I share some of the rough spots of my childhood with my closest friends I am certain that it is God I answer to, because if it were not for my faith I would not be alive. I am just foolish enough to believe that God does not care so much what I wear as what I do for others. God is not caught up in the sound of my voice, but God is the content of the message I am instructed to deliver. There is an African proverb that says, "It is not important what we are called but to what we answer." I have been called and will be called many names by those who do not like or do not agree with me and also many names by those who love and support me. I recognize that my name is not slut, gal, whore, crazy, stupid, great, bishop, or queen but God's daughter, Teresa. This is the name to which I eternally answer. This is the name that enables me to continue doing ministry.

I recall the words I gleaned reading Anna Julia Cooper's book in the fall of 1987. Three concepts, grounded in the biblical text, are essential to the self-empowerment work that frames my life and my work with women in ministry today:[7]

One must love one's self. God loves me, and if I do not love myself enough to care for my own ministry then I have denied that love. If I do not love myself I am unable to have energy to genuinely love others.

One must have self-control. We are responsible for how we live, what we say, and how we engage others. We must eliminate a debilitating victim mentality. Yes, we have all had our trials, but we have to move on at some point. We can participate in our own demise by constant referring to what could have been or should have been.

To a great extent, *one is responsible for determining the course of one's life.* Certainly we each face hierarchies, rules, regulations, pecking orders, cliques, committees, boards, panels, covenants, and accrediting institutions. Playing the stereotypic "weak" woman to please "strong" men, using exclusive theological language to avoid criticism, or employing coy, babygirl voices to gain pseudo-privileges diminishes all who struggled for ecclesiastical equality. We also have a choice in how much of our life we are willing to sign over to them. We may become complicit in the minimal progression of our ministries when we spend all our time waiting in line for someone to tell us when to speak, when to laugh, how high to jump, when to

---

7. Cooper, *A Voice from the South,* 9–45.

roll over, and when to play dead. Constant self-deprecation or over-solicitousness ("Oh, but I'm (only) a woman") is an embarrassment to contemporary women and desecrates the legacy of all the women who came before us. We live in collectivity, but at the end of the road we stand by ourselves.

MOTHER WIT AND SISTAH SENSE

Reverend sister girlfriend, listen to what they never tell you in seminary or the church—Mother Wit and Sistah Sense truisms, musings, and lessons on womanly self-expression:

1. Language is power; use it wisely.
2. Sticks and stones do break emotional bones.
3. Your voice is distinctive. Try not to use, imitate, or borrow someone else's.
4. Tell your own story.
5. Remember that you too are made in the image of God.
6. It may be church, but remember the people came from outside.
7. Church games and church names kill.
8. Cry when you feel like it. Jesus did. People did not understand him at first either.
9. We are not exempt from pain, fear, distress, anger, disappointment, anxiety, confusion, or any other so-called negative emotion that can silence us.
10. When the pressure builds up, find a safe place—a room, your car, a field—some place where you can shout, scream, cry, talk, whisper, curse, or whatever gets the toxic stuff out of your system.
11. Whatever it was yesterday, get over it today.
12. If we have an attitude about something, it is often deeply rooted and not just "that time of the month."
13. Listen to your elders. They have been where you are attempting to go.

14. Never let anyone know all of your thoughts; spiritual plagiarism is real.
15. Never follow anyone less intelligent than you.
16. Sometimes a sister just needs her space; don't take it personally.
17. If you have lost you, it's time for a road trip, scavenger hunt, or something to pick up your pieces.
18. Take time for a reality check at least once a week, particularly when you are having misgivings about ministry or something someone asked you to do.
19. If you can't say it, partner with a sister who can.
20. Do the research before you speak.
21. A wise woman never knows all; only fools know everything (adapted African proverb).
22. Lack of response does not mean your idea was not accepted. Perhaps it was simply too deep for an immediate reaction.
23. Remember that not every woman in ministry is your friend.
24. Black women do not perspire or glisten. We sweat. Always prepare yourself before and after a sermon for water to cascade. Avoid silk or any fabric that will shrink when it is wet.
25. There is always more material in the store and a larger size. Do not believe the sales woman who says something looks nice and yet you cannot breathe.
26. Invest in good hosiery that matches your skin tone. Nothing looks worse than beige elephant ankle wrinkles on dark brown skin. Carry an extra pair in your bag.
27. Be prepared for body microphones. Take a belt or wear something with pockets. Sometimes, depending on your bust measurement, the microphone may get lost or bounce around a lot. Placing a microphone on the waistband of your skirt or slacks may mean a dropped microphone when you stand up.

28. There are some sisters who do not like or cannot afford or understand that not everyone looks good in St. John knits. Caveat: Knit can only stretch so much; then it no longer hangs attractively but screams for immediate relief.

29. Wear the skirt length that is most comfortable for you. Your mother or someone else along the way taught you how to sit so that a big blanket would not be necessary to "hide your modesty." (If men would also wear a lap cloth to hide the visible evidence of their gender, then I might consider it!)

30. You have spent more time with your body than anyone, so pay attention to it.

In your quest to express yourself, God has given you a mind, a memory, and a mouth. You perceived a special mental communication from God to which you alone were privileged. Rely on the synapses in that mind to figure out where your ministry is to go next. Exercise that mind to formulate the power to do the impossible. Think about where you have been and what you have already accomplished, and know that God promised not to leave you without a support system. Finally, use the power of speech to answer not only to humans but to God through the language of faith. God has given you enough power for the journey. Do not give it away.

Girl, do you realize how long we've been on this phone? How many minutes do you have? I know you have to call your girl back. I believe Lynn will be alright if we all support her. No, girl, they're just upset because she can speak a complete sentence with subject-verb agreement. I'm supposed to be working on a sermon. I'll holla' at you later. Tell the family I said Hello. Love ya, too.

I'm out,
T

THREE

HORMONAL SHIFTS

Alright, Sistergirls,

It's time to get up close and personal. I know we do not like to talk about our bodies and minds but someone has to start the conversation.

You know how we run around pretending to be well because ministers are not supposed to have any problems and, evidently, few emotions? After all, we represent not only God but all the sisters who ever walked this way. We, as women, do not want to be thought weak or unable to do the work because "it's that time," or because we will cry in response to something. I would not cry in the pulpit or at funerals for years because I did not want to be challenged with doing "that woman thing." God had another plan.

The commentator predictably reported that the ten-year-old girl and her eleven-year-old brother were the future Olympic figure skating pairs champions. The competition had been tough. They needed to achieve at least two 9.5 scores or higher for their last routine. The TV showed the perfunctory life-at-home shots, an interview with the beaming parents, talk of the sacrifices the other siblings had made for this precocious pair, and some replays of their previous performances. They entered the rink in color-coordinated outfits to the thunderous cheers of the crowd. All the lights except two spots dimmed. The first strains of carefully selected performance music wafted from invisible suspended speakers. They smiled and clasped hands. They slowly began to take synchronized steps on the frigid dance floor.

I was supposed to be writing a research paper but it was Saturday afternoon and the week had been difficult. I was taking an unscheduled break so I joined my daughter, Veronica, who was watching *Wide World of Sports* in the living room. I was tired and irritable but the sight of the children made me smile. They were executing the choreographed compulsory movements brilliantly given their age. I have watched ice skating since Sister Debi Thomas represented us in the 1988 Olympics. I was certain these two would qualify easily. Just as they initiated the toe loop in the final combination the little girl stumbled, tried to right herself, spun awkwardly, and fell flat on her butt. I am not sure who started wailing first, the little skater or me. She sat there for a few seconds looking down—although it seemed longer. The camera, of course, panned to the faces of the concerned parents. The commentator began the obligatory replay of the fall and analysis accompanied by the prediction that the pair would receive low scores. Fighting off his own disappointment, the little girl's brother helped her up as she straightened her skirt. The crowd began to applaud. The siblings finished the program, bravely smiling while knowing they were out of the competition.

I must have been sobbing for about five minutes when my child said, "Mom, they have medicine for that!"

The brain is an awesome organ. We have the amazing ability to think about more than one thing at a time. We can integrate past, present, and anticipated experiences while expending relatively little physical energy. At the time of my life when I watched this pair of skaters, I was on an emotional edge trying to balance work, bills, motherhood, school, church, and a little time for myself. I cried at church. I cried at school. I cried at home. I cried in the car. I cried watching commercials. I cried watching the sun set behind the mountains. I must have been crying off and on for about three months without obvious provocation. I grew up around boys and was taught that only "girly girls" cry.

That particular afternoon, watching TV with my daughter, it took me an hour to figure out what, other than the child's skating mishap, had triggered my spontaneous Niagara Falls imitation. That little girl sitting on the ice subconsciously became a metaphor for my ministry journey.

My entrance into ministry had been touted as the opening of the brick ceiling. I became part of the promise that "sons and daughters would prophesy." My home church was viewed as "the place" for women in ministry. The senior pastor was appointed to the African Methodist Episcopal Church General Board Women in Ministry Committee. My family endured many sacrifices because I was working about eighteen hours per day preparing to be the best minister God intended me to be. Congregants, family, and other ministers were counting on me to be a "star."

So I was under constant scrutiny. I felt as if a panel of "experts in the field" were judging every mazurka hairstyle, one-footed axel shoe selection, double lutz Bible study, triple Salchow worship leadership, quad toe loop sermon, and flying camel visitations in my repertoire. I sensed I was the plot line in a George Orwellian doomsday novel. My entire life was on display for the Wide World of Ministry channel surfers. I kept waiting for one of them to give me a "0.0" instead of a 9.5 or higher.

My descent to expulsion or my ascent to the finals seemed to be in someone else's hands. Didn't they know how hard I had trained for ministry? Didn't they care? How did they feel when they were on the ice? Who would be there to help me up and fix my clothes? Could I really finish the program?

I was also becoming an emotional wreck. One misspoken word, one missed meeting, one messed-up protocol step, one misinterpreted ministry moment and I thought I would fall flat on my butt in the middle of the "frozen chosen," with no one to rush in and help me stand up and continue my program. I always had possessed some control over my emotions, especially in public, but had reached the point that even sunshine made me weep.

I decided to consider my child's recommendation. I made appointments with my doctors to try to get some medicine to stop the leak. The initial diagnosis was that I was experiencing hormonal shifts. I had lived through two years of abdominal pain, unpredictable emotions, and extremely heavy menses. After three weeks of tests I was diagnosed with *the* Black women's gynecological problem, multiple fibroid tumors. Surgery was the last resort. The doctor first opted for hormone therapy. Having been treated for early stage cancer in my late twenties, I had some additional concerns now as a thirty-eight-year-old divorced single mother.

But I did have normal concerns. I identified with the woman with the issue of blood. Although I used more backup systems than Microsoft, one of my reverend sister friends did a sight check of my robes whenever I stood up. This was harrowing, particularly on each first Sunday of the month when ministers are required to wear white. Yet that was a minor irritant compared to the flawed rationale that women's hormonal shifts preclude them from sustained effective ministry in general.

My emotional roller coaster did not stop. My symptoms worsened and surgery was scheduled. I knew I had to tell my pastor. He had informed me in my first year of ministry that I was not to cry in the pulpit because people would think I was weak. We had had several conversations regarding my emotional state.

As the senior associate, I eventually had to inform ministerial colleagues and church leadership of my anticipated absence for surgery so they could arrange adequate ministry coverage while I was away.

What do I remember about people's responses? The most memorable responses ran the gamut from asinine to empathetic. "Your voice will change." "You will grow a beard." "My mother told me that the reason it is called a hysterectomy is because after the surgery women become hysterical." "If you let them open you up you will get cancer." "No man wants half a woman." "Well, it's a good thing you have Veronica, because this means no more children." Others told me, "Girl, you will love it," and "You will finally be free." Still others insisted, "You are going to get *fat*," or, more sympathetically, "Join the club." My immediate thought was that if the leaders voiced these morsels of "wisdom," what would the congregation say? Some had witnessed my crying jags but counted them as "spirit" endowed.

I knew that there were those who accepted the myth that women should not be in pulpits because they will defile the pulpit during menstruation. I was now in my fifth month of hormonal hell, yet the church was not quarantined, infected, or dead. Yet when on the day before my surgery I announced from the pulpit that I was scheduled to have a hysterectomy and asked for prayers, there were the predictable collective knots of gasps and many whispers. I did not want rumors to circulate that I was pregnant or aborting. Sometimes sisters have to preempt a mess later by airing personal laundry now.

God works in mysterious ways. The funniest part of all of this is that upon my return to church the men would not hug me because they thought they would hurt me. It took about two months until things returned to normal. Well, not exactly normal. While I was recuperating the senior pastor encountered some deeply emotional issues. The no crying in the pulpit sign came down. Handkerchiefs came out. Men and women were free to cry without critique, at least by the other ministers. It took six months before my hormones were regularized through natural and synthetic therapies. It took another year of education to overcome gossip about my surgery and several more years to derail the thought that if a minister is sick she has sinned more than anyone else.

Just in case you were wondering, I did not grow a beard. I did not gain an inordinate amount of weight. Nor did I lose interest in men or men in me. I did not languish in a hysterical state for years. I did, however, feel a new sense of freedom, particularly on first Sundays. And in the years since then, the harder part continues to be managing the external forces that impact my emotions. I cling to the knowledge that Jesus, the Son of God, was human enough to cry and I am wholly human and wholly woman made in the image of God. I no longer watch figure skating but do at times cry watching the news, Black history documentaries, legal dramas, and even occasionally commercials. I no longer make up excuses for compassion or hormones. I seek the corrective to my healing from trusted sources. I follow the prescriptions even when I find medicine minimally palatable. That whole pruning, molding, and making thing in ministry was and is difficult to take when I am in the midst of emotional, spiritual, or physical wounds. When I look back, though, I appreciate even the hardest lessons.

What else have I learned? That the lives of women in ministry are a curious intermingling of poignant disruption paired with delightful immovability. At any point in time we may have to negotiate a tightrope walk through sickness and health, hurts and pains, trials and tribulations, joys and blessings, and life and death. We may find ourselves placidly doing the work of the one who sent us, then suddenly being blindsided by personal or interpersonal issues. At other times all the lights are green, there is no speed limit posted, and the tank is full of gas. Nothing seems to stop our progress and unfettered joy washes over our souls.

But other times our lack of good health holds us back. To say that Black women do not attend to their own health because we are so busy making sure everyone else is taken care of would be a gross understatement. Yet, when we are not feeling well, no one feels well. Imbalance, malice, dysfunction, confusion, and fear reign. Simply put, when we are sick, our ministry suffers. The more we push on in spite of the illness, the more we miss. I am not talking about chronic or catastrophic illness. (I have known women who worked right up to the time of death. I cannot critique their choice but I wonder what other things they could have done with that time. Jesus had a dinner at least!) I am talking about acute illness that a visit to the doctor would begin to remedy. After all, when we have adequate mental, physical, emotional, and spiritual health, we can help someone else. What kind of example do we set if we do not seek to "heal ourselves"? Remember, to be called a martyr means you have died for something. Choose wisely.

Attention to our physical health is one important aspect of ministry. Attention to our theology is another. Ministers may have a different theology, a different understanding of who God is and how God works, than the congregation. It may in fact be our beliefs and not our gender that prompts our being attacked or ostracized. We verbally retaliate because someone said someone else said something and no one has the facts straight. Listen: Everyone, including you, can have an opinion. It does not mean you have to like it, but it is just that: someone's opinion. So assess the church culture and locate your allies. Maintain perspective. Do not declare war unless there are really "weapons formed against you," then pray for guidance before you contribute to the destruction of the faith community. If, for example, you believe God created *all* persons equal regardless of their gender, class, race, ethnicity, sexuality, physical ability, health, or martial status and the church leadership membership does not, then it's time to consider your options. Depending on the polity of the church you can quit, fight, teach, or assimilate. No need to blow up, cuss, scream, fall out, or revert to some preconversion language and action. You are an adult. There are other places of worship. Exercise the option that works for you. In the Book it says, "avoid stupid controversies, genealogies, dissensions, and quarrels about the law, for they are unprofitable and worthless" (Titus 3:9). If none of the options work, shake the dust off your feet and move on. Aren't you glad you are not doing the same things you did when you began this journey?

It's beguiling to lose yourself in arguments and assumptions. It takes discipline and character to hold back, stay steady, and speak the truth. Though folks say, "Age ain't nothing but a number," early on in my ministry I got hooked into silly debates about age. Until I was granted tenure I was the oldest female "junior" faculty member at my seminary. Many days I bemoaned my "lost" years. I thought about how much I could be doing if I had I answered the call earlier. I occasionally became despondent anticipating aging and grieved the thought of my body slowing down. I lamented the possibility of losing the power in my voice and mourned the potential of a decrease in mental sharpness. Yes, I buried myself in societal myths about aging. Yet as I conversed with younger first-career women entering ministry I grew to appreciate how much life experience helps one navigate the rough seas of ministry. These younger saints helped me get in touch with how every second of my life prepared me for where I am right now. I accept my status as older sister and in some cases the other mother. Most of what they are going through I passed through some time ago.

There is something to this whole "seasoned saint" idea. There are few things that now shock me. I may be surprised but not shocked. I am able to take most critiques with aplomb. I still have pain but it does not hurt as much as it used to hurt. I fall back on the lessons of my mothers, grandmothers, and other mothers when they said, "They may kill your body but not your soul." I try to reserve my anger, disappointment, sorrow, and righteous indignation for life-and-death matters. When my sisters tell me they cannot do something because of their age I say, "How much older will you be if you don't do it?"

Too many of us carry around such extra baggage. Each bag is engraved with the nature, date, and place of past offenses. Each bag is filled with our "used to's," "shoulda, coulda, woulda's," and "if I had's." We do not go any place without the extra baggage. We willingly pay extra for the overage yet complain about the annoyance of transporting it all with us. A simple quarterly closet cleaning will allow us to travel faster and lighter. Whatever we are holding onto needs to be discarded and not retrieved or else we'll become entombed in our past. We must confront the guilt and shame of who we were before we entered ministry. We have to let go of what others know about us. Secrets are transitory. There is always someone who will betray a confidence innocently or blatantly. Ministry does not mean we are instantly pure and holy, just humans called to a higher standard of living. Let go of the baggage.

I think back to my early years of ministry, of being perpetually angry after meeting with congregants and staff. I felt my blood pressure rise just thinking about talking with some people. Evidently, lay people think that ministers don't (or shouldn't) get mad even though members of the laity can be demonic and dismissive. So I walked around with a fake smile and muttered a clenched-teeth "God bless you." My family did not understand why I did not just tell the people off. "Do they know who you are and what you do when someone treats you like that? I wouldn't take that from anybody. Ministry has made you a punk," they told me, irritated.

Congregational critiques do not always begin with what you would understand as a negative situation. One Sunday I was having one of those "caught up to meet God" kind of days. I love to worship God and I worship with my whole heart. At some point in the service I was overcome with the Spirit and was later told I danced out of my shoes and was laid out in the pulpit for awhile. I was feeling wonderful until my phone rang later that afternoon. "My mom said you were just acting crazy today. You embarrassed her. She said you would explain what happened." I had just experienced true liberation through worship and with one phone call the chains were back on me. There was no getting away from my captors. I patiently tried to explain to the child about being endowed by God's Spirit. I then asked to speak to her mother and did the same. The mother told me she was not raised with people shouting and dancing in church and did not understand it. She thought my conduct was unbecoming for a woman. I was civil but the conversation added another ounce of venom to tuck away in my women-in-ministry-have-to-take-all-affronts baggage. I was beginning to exceed the weight allowances for travel.

When I just could not take it anymore I asked for a meeting with the senior pastor. I had talked with some of my sisters in ministry but I knew I had to go to the head of the congregation. He used to call me at ungodly hours like 5:30 A.M. to ask me to do things for the church, so I figured he could take time to hear about the church from my perspective. He said he had about fifteen minutes open on his schedule. I insisted I needed at least an hour. Following prayer I gave him a typed copy of my agenda. I began reading bullet points off my legal pad. I found it expeditious to write down my points so if I cried or became angry I could find my place and still manage to convey everything I had on my mind. And if we ran out of time he would have a written copy of my information whether he ever read it or not.

Well, after the fifth point I blew a gasket. He sat there with a Cheshire cat grin on his face, which just made me angrier. I wanted to slap him out of that chair. Then the man had the nerve to start laughing. "They've got you just where they want you," he said. I blurted out: "What in the world is wrong with you? These people don't know me. I want to knock them into next week, but nooooo, I have to be quiet because I'm a preacher. Just one minute, I want just one minute in a room with them." Then he really started laughing and said, "Who told you that? You can stand up for yourself. But whatever you do, make sure you will remain in a position to do ministry. Probably

they're actually mad about something else entirely, and this may
be their only place to feel powerful. They think because you are
supposed to be closer to God you can take it."

He then began to tell of his early years in ministry and those
times when the same people who attacked him in meetings
called him to come pray for them in hospitals, counsel them in
failing marriages, or help get a loved one out of jail as if nothing
negative had ever happened between them. He advised me to
listen past what people were saying to me and try to find a ministry moment. He also told me to go to my car, roll all the windows up and cuss for all I was worth, then continue my work. To
this day I'm not sure I buy all of his rationale. He was my elder
in ministry and no doubt he had had experiences I would never
have. But he was also a male, and it's simply the truth that congregants respond differently to ministers based on gender and
age. To this day I genuinely think some people are just mean. I
know that I am instructed to pray for even my enemies. It is
hard, but I am trying to remain faithful to all aspects of my call.

Now listen: Who knows you better than you? You are the
best monitor of your own emotional state. Yet a healthy self-
critique is essential to the success of our ministry. I know that
some of us have a Messiah complex and believe that nothing
will happen without us there. So we exhaust ourselves and then
blame others for our fatigue. When we fail to set manageable
goals and objectives, we face burnout. Knowing this, I run a
self-assessment every month or so. I review my problem-solving
skills, organizational management abilities, academic and ecclesial obligations, family time, and care of self. I have to be real-
istic about what I can and cannot complete. So I prioritize. And
I have learned to write letters, make calls, or send e-mails to
request extensions or cancellations. I suggest substitutes when
asked. I know when I am sick, and I am learning to listen to my
body. I am a perfectionist. I know that I am not perfect but set
high standards for myself. I try to give my best at all times. If I
am functioning at only one-fourth of my ability, I ask to be ex-

cused. I do not like to make apologies for my public presentations; either I am prepared or I am not prepared. No excuses. I do not want to embarrass myself, but, more important, I always want to give God my best.

Our emotional health is affected by everyday church life. We form emotional attachments to the congregation as a whole or to particular members of it. In the body of Christ the pain of one reaches more than the immediate family. Loss of relationship, job, health, or positions impacts our approach to the people and how we minister with them. We mourn with the people as replays of other divorces, downsizings, disagreements, and deaths hover around the edges of our thoughts. We celebrate life passages with the people as remembrances of other births, graduations, baptisms, weddings, ordinations, promotions, and sometimes funerals elevate our visions.

The rituals and routines of ministry stir up sentiment. The liturgical calendar and special days help us recall the foundations of our faith. They also may unearth painful or wonderful times in our lives that impinge on our present situation. My least favorite holiday is Christmas, not the Jesus-is-born caroling part but the human celebrative part. In my childhood my parents were stressed until Christmas morning with whether or not they could manage to buy each of their seven children a toy. There were always people in and out of the house who cared more about toasting the season than the reason for it. There was the fear that someone would displace their anger at being Black in America for a chance to argue and fight at Christmas dinner. I was sometimes humiliated and sometimes happy for that basket of fruit and ribbon candy the missionary society would leave on our porch.

So now in my adulthood I approach holidays with cautious awareness that if I am not careful all those childhood memories, particularly the most violent ones, will surface during the chorus of "Joy to the World" and I will dissolve into a pool of tears. I have to distract myself by being super busy at minute tasks or playing games with my friends until the urge passes or the season ends.

Another ritual that I've learned can undo my best intentions is the fellowship meal or potluck. Food is one of those guilty pleasures that levels the playing field. Having cooked and served many conference and special day dinners before I entered ministry and several since, although I know that church food is a ministry for some, I have had to take control of my own well-being in order to run faster and farther. I eat only what I know I need. If there is a request to "Make sure you get some of my _____," I take a small portion just to taste it. I request that I have no spicy food. I usually do not eat before I preach. If I preach a night service, I do not go to bed immediately after returning to the hotel room. I exercise or work for an hour or two. I now have enough voice to share my dietary needs with the mothers of the church. They have been fabulous about making sure I am eating right. There have been a few who asked if I was sick, if I hated their food, or why I avoid pork. I would love to be able to eat what I want, when I want it, but the truth is that has never been the case. As my mother used to say, there is a difference between want and need. I need to be healthy. So I am careful about what I eat.

I cook only on Sundays, holidays, and about two days per week due to a rather hectic schedule. When I have time, I find making fresh bread or cobblers or creating some new dish to be relaxing. I enjoy the taste, aroma, and feel of food. My soul feels good after a good meal. In the words of my daughter, some food just "makes me happy." Yet doesn't it seem that each pleasure has a caveat? We women in ministry must be selective about what and when we eat. One of the difficulties of church life is convincing well-meaning congregants of dietary concerns. Some place in time our church culture decided that abundant food or fellowship meals was a way of showing appreciation, extending hospitality, and deciding the best cook in a spiritual culinary contest. If there is a special day, there will be food. Churches serve elaborate breakfasts between services, place baskets of fruit, candy, or snacks in hotel rooms, or insist on us attending several dinners. I love each of the amenities. If I do not accept a heaping plate of home-cooked food lovingly prepared for me and served by the mothers of the church I will offend every Black woman who has ever attended a church. Sister Sense tells me, however, that if I eat everything on my plate or eat too late my body will rebel. Yes, there are those times when I splurge or fall off the no-chocolate-no-pork-no-salty-foods wagon, but I do not feel guilty about it. At the end of the day I cannot allow food to become my emotional crutch or my depravation. I am the one who ultimately has to care for my body. I will not be loved to death by food. The beauty of table fellowship is that the community comes together as family.

Another affirming ritual is Holy Communion, or Holy Eucharist, or the Lord's Supper. It is the ritual that most profoundly affects my spiritual life. It is a ritual of deep holiness and humanity. I believe that there is Spirit power in the reenactment of that Last Supper. It helps me move past personal and interpersonal betrayal to forgiveness and ultimately to thanksgiving. I am reminded that Jesus' ministry was not widely accepted. It is Jesus' model of ministry in spite of and on behalf of others that floods the depths of my spiritual, emotional, and psychological being, and I am encouraged to keep on trying to do my assigned tasks. When rituals are done as worship and not as performance, I find comfort and healing in them regardless of the voices that present them. I am particularly taken to a different place when a child who is new to the faith walk or an elder who has long tenure on the faith walk is the liturgist, speaker, or preacher. Whatever provides a place for expression of and healing for our emotions is what we should employ to continue on our way.

MOTHER WIT AND SISTAH SENSE

Reverend sister girlfriend, listen to what they never tell you in seminary or the church—Mother Wit and Sistah Sense truisms, musings, and lessons on shifting hormones and managing emotions:

1. The sister who walks to the beat of her own drum may be expelled from the orchestra, but she can start her own band.
2. Taking risks is part of life. How did you learn to walk in the first place?
3. Ostracism, alienation, and resistance from human judges are part of the package. No one can guarantee a slide up the mountain, just a quick fall down if your soul and feet are not anchored.
4. Engage evil and she will leave you alone at least for a few days.
5. Allow room for mistakes. No one is perfect.
6. Take care of your body. God only gave us one temple.
7. Always get a second, third, or fourth opinion if necessary.
8. Walk, run, crawl, hop, skip, jump, roll on by faith, employing any means necessary for forward progress.
9. Choose your battles wisely. Fighting on all fronts at all times depletes your resilience. You will bleed to death before the most important encounters. Reverend sister, sharing and delegating battles means winning the entire war and not just one or two battles.
10. Block out white noise and listen for the move of God in your life. We are surrounded by so many people claiming to know what God said that it is difficult at times to know what God really said. Listen to your inner voice.
11. Welcome both the small steps and the lasting leaps. Our foremothers were correct when they said you have to crawl before you walk. I know we get in a hurry, but some things really do take time.
12. Develop contemplative practices such as daily meditation and prayer, not just in public but in your own space and time at home.
13. Live what you say you know and believe. Sisters cannot play dress-up forever.

14. It is better to walk alone than to be consumed by toxic relationships. It's over. Move on before you start corroding.

15. Respites, sabbaticals, Sabbaths, and solitude are critical. I have a sign on my home office door that says, "Woman at work. Don't even think about disturbing me."

16. Don't take yourself too seriously. No one is that holy. You were not asked to get up on the cross; someone already did that job.

17. Find and keep a good doctor and a mental health professional. Unless you really graduated from an accredited medical school, completed an internship and residency, passed all your tests, took the do-no-harm oath, and have an established practice at a real office or hospital, *do not self-diagnose*. This will save you hours of anguish. I know you are afraid, so take someone to the real doctor with you.

18. Take the medicine, all of the medicine, on schedule as prescribed.

19. The choice is yours: exercise one hour a day or be dead twenty-four hours a day.

20. Even when the senior pastor and congregation gets on that last nerve, keep yourself in a place of ministry.

21. Set boundaries: end the "superwoman" (strong Black woman) syndrome.

22. Allocate space for healthy catharsis or a release valve for pent-up emotions: cry, scream, talk, run, dance, call a real friend—whatever works for you.

23. Play, play, play, play, play.

24. Laugh, laugh, laugh, laugh, laugh.

25. Read something other than ministry stuff.

26. Key into the power of your imagination.

27. Relish "How I Got Over" moments.

28. Forgive yourself and others.

29. Sleep on it.

30. Know when to say when, enough is enough, no more, that's all folks.

31. Victory is in the start, not necessarily when or where you finish.

32. Technology is a blessing. Take advantage of call waiting, e-mail, and caller ID. They allow you space to heal, think, rest, create, or play.

33. Study—learning and teaching. Try to learn at least one new word, skill, or bit of information every day.

34. Sometimes acting crazy is a good move. It keeps people out of your space.

35. Get rid of *all* excess baggage.

The biblical text puts it this way: "Let us also lay aside every weight . . . and run with perseverance the race set before us, looking to Jesus the pioneer and perfecter of our faith. . . ." (Heb. 12:1b–2a). The good news according to Dr. T (that would be me) puts it this way: "Call the coroner. Schedule the autopsy. Arrange for flowers. Hold the funeral. Bury the memory. Never exhume that pain, person, place, position, procedure, or promise again in life. Jesus says, *"I've* got this," so keep on running and don't even think about looking back.

My sisters, I do not expect you to use all of the things I have shared. I do know, however, that each of us has experienced something that has left us sick, tired, questioning, or confused about our ministry or our health. So I end this portion of our conversation with "God's Multi-faceted Healing Power," which I composed in 2003 for a women's retreat in Houston, Texas. As a former speech, hearing, and language pathologist and current teacher of preaching, I was invited to present one workshop on finding one's voice and one on faith and healing. The purpose of each workshop was to encourage women to take responsibility for their own healing under the power of God's unction. Here it is:

GOD'S MULTIFACETED HEALING POWER

LEADER: Jehovah Rapha, Our Healer, you told us to always pray and not give up.

PEOPLE: Jehovah Rapha, Our Healer, teach us how to pray. Teach us to pray when we are doing well and when we are in need. Jehovah Rapha, Our Healer, empower us to continue to pray when you say yes, when you say no, and when you say wait.

LEADER: Jehovah Rapha, Our Liberator, when you took on all our sins, you said the prayers of the faithful would change lives and situations.

PEOPLE: Jehovah Rapha, Our Liberator, help us to see you in the midst of the death, destruction, disease, and disappointment of this world so that we may one day realize your kin-dom, your reign of interrelationship, here on earth.

LEADER: Jehovah Rapha, Our Great Physician, touch the deep hurts, pains, and prejudices that threaten our physical, mental, emotional, psychological, and spiritual bodies this day.

PEOPLE: Jehovah Rapha, Our Great Physician, pour the oil of salvation and your healing balm into our woundedness, reset all the fractured and fragmented relationships with our brothers and sisters, and impregnate our self-destructive views with the nourishing seeds of your love.

LEADER: Jehovah Rapha, Our Transformer, because you love us, you prevent hurt, harm, and danger from destroying our bodies, souls, and minds.

PEOPLE: Jehovah Rapha, Our Transformer, keep your arms of protection around us so that human-made weapons never kill our souls and minds, so that we stand firm on your promises, and so we can fly with eagles' wings above the stuff that threatens to lead us off the path of righteousness.

LEADER: Jehovah Rapha, Our Reconciler, continue to nurture us, feed us, connect us, correct us, lead us, direct us, love us, and intercede for us as we grow in faith and live in your grace and mercy.

ALL: *Jehovah Rapha, Our Reconciler, guide our minds and tongues as we accept the power of healing in acknowledgment of who you are and in thanksgiving for all you have done. Help us to* pray for *rather than* prey on *one another so that each of us may be healed in spirit, mind, body, and relationships.*[1]

We women are more than the sum total of our hormones. Our chemical-based emotional action and reaction may be used as an excuse for others to bar us from ministry or for us to move past a mistake. We are more than estrogen containers. Every part of us is fully human, not a mistake or a punishment. If we do not care for ourselves, no one else will. With or without tears, cramps, periods, or uncontrolled laughter we need to live into the passage in Philippians 3:13, "I can do all things through [God] who strengthens me" as we press on toward the goal of our calls. We are not weak, whether we laugh or cry. Facing a world filled with callous, critical, cruel, cantankerous, and caustic men and women, I feel blessed that some of us still feel compassion. Break out the tissues. Our healing is on the way.

Love,

T

---

1. Teresa L. Fry Brown, composed for a women's conference at Brookhollow Baptist Church, Houston, Texas, 2003.

FOUR

✳

STUMBLING BLOCKS AND SAFETY NETS

✳

My Sisters in God's Service,

I've got good news and I've got bad news. There are innumerable women and men willing and able to give encouragement and advice to anyone who asks. However, finding a support system can be one of the most rewarding or one of the most disarming parts of sustaining your ministry. We may begin a relationship with a mentor who provides a safety net for us but over time becomes a stumbling block. A stumbling block is anything or anyone, including ourselves, that slows, blocks, or (temporarily or permanently) impedes our progress. I think of a safety net as anything or anyone, including ourselves, that envelops, supports, protects, or (temporarily or permanently) enhances our advancement. Stumbling blocks or safety nets materialize in the form of oneself, children, spouses, siblings, family, congregants, colleagues, ministers, or friends. Careful consideration, thoughtful selectivity, and patient understanding are essential for avoiding stumbling blocks and reserving safety nets.

When I go to a restaurant, I look at the dessert menu before I look at the entrees. Somehow I find comfort in knowing that my reward is coming if I eat all my vegetables and choice of protein. I like the anticipation of a silky chocolate mousse or a sugar encrusted vanilla crème brulée.

That is generally how I face life. I know it is sometimes about priority and sometimes about balance. I want to deal with the unsavory matter first, then move on unencumbered to the satisfying things. As we labor through the who, what, when, where, why, and how of ministry, we prayerfully ask God for the discernment to identify the stumbling blocks and the safety nets. I believe it is only through provision and direction from God that we will survive the struggles of "Hold me back, girl" and the security of "God's got this."

As you may have gathered by now, I am a fighter. I don't mean I try to raise hell because I do not have anything else to do. I struggle to survive and to thrive. At the end of my life I do not want to say, "If only I had . . ." or "I couldn't because. . . ."

I was raised by the men in my family to take care of myself, not to rely on anyone to do anything that I could do myself, and never to let people walk over me, no matter who they were or thought they were.

I was taught by the women in my family to love everyone, not necessarily what a person did or had done; to be a lady (meaning clothes clean and pressed, hair combed, no holes anywhere, dress down, legs together, no public cursing, no chewing with my mouth open, and so on); and to love God.

Both the men and the women taught me that one of my greatest personal safety nets and one of my greatest stumbling blocks is me. They believed in survival of the fittest through cultivation of the gifts and talents God instilled within us. They gave me the tools to succeed by their example and values.

Preservation and perpetuation of their basic cultural values have been a lifesaver to me on this course.[1]

We are responsible for our own lives. No one can live them for us. So why spend such an inordinate amount of time blaming others for our situations? The choices we make are just that: choices. Whether they are right or wrong, they are our choices and we must live with the consequences. I was taught to have reverence for God and for my elders. I honor God because of God's creative force and love. I honor my elders because they broke the path, took the brunt of the hatred, and provided for my present. My elders instructed that even if society does not esteem me because of my skin color, gender, belief, or residence, I have an obligation to respect myself.

My elders also taught me about reciprocity: I do for others not only because they have done something for me but simply because it is the right thing to do. Someone someplace without my knowledge helped me. They did not believe in ignoring those in need, often allowing houseless people or children experiencing problems at home to live with them for months and years. They did not believe that anyone should be hungry and so they always found a way to feed extra mouths. They did not brag about what they had done, insist it be published in the paper, or announced at church. They taught me to have restraint and control. They taught me that everything or everyone who is good to us is not necessarily also good for us. We must know when to say when and stand by that decision. Finally, my elders taught me to live life with a hopeful expectation that, as my late mentor, Jesse Langston Boyd, would say, "The ground is level at the foot of the cross." Each person, regardless of perceived or ascribed human power, must eventually answer for her life. My elders told me—and through experience I have learned—that my failure to em-

1. For an extensive treatment of African American cultural values, see Teresa Fry Brown, *God Don't Like Ugly: African American Women Handing on Spiritual Values* (Nashville: Abingdon Press, 2000).

ploy these basic tenets will mean failure of my safety net and the certainty of extensive personal injury.

The support or lack of support from the family has a tremendous effect on a minister. Family members, while not answering your call, are placed under scrutiny by association. My daughter, who was two when I entered ordained ministry, was called a "preacher's kid," a child whose parent's profession automatically means they are either considered to be dysfunctional and promiscuous, or are afforded the rights and privileges of royalty. There was an expectation that my daughter, Veronica, would be either a spoiled brat or needed extra protection. My child rearing was critiqued no matter what. I was a no-nonsense mother. Veronica thought since I was in the pulpit I either would not see her or would not stop what I was doing in worship to correct her behavioral indiscretions. After a few times of my descending the pulpit during a song and having a real mother-daughter chat in the bathroom, she understood that minister moms multitask. Some members of the congregation began warning her the moment they noticed I was watching her. Her auntie Richelle took her out of the sanctuary and chastised her when I was not able to stop what I was doing and be the hands-on mom. For years I was fortunate to have an extended family that would intercept Veronica when I drove into the church parking lot and who watched her until it was time for us to go home. If I had to travel, preach, or do unexpected hospital visitations, they would make sure she ate, slept, and did her homework.

Veronica's life has been complicated by having a mother who was an "exception to the rule." She has heard things about me that she will not tell me. (I am not sure if she thinks it will hurt me too much or if she is just too overcome to repeat the bad stuff.) She often voices her disdain of the church, choosing as an adult not to attend from time to time, because of her understanding of faith, ministry, racial equality, and women's rights. She has been inculcated to become a womanist through her contact with my colleagues in the church and the academy. I have apologized to her in my guilty mommy moments for those times I was unable to be present at some event because I was on the road. I am always humbled when she says, "Mom, you did a good job. I turned out alright. Besides, you were doing what God told you to do." She is one of my loudest cheerleaders and supporters and I am grateful. I also realize that there are many who do not have that same experience with their children. God gave me one for a reason. I cannot fathom how women are able to do ministry and raise several children, most of the time as single mothers. My shoes (since I rarely wear hats!) are off to you, my sisters.

Our call to ministry affects the beliefs and lives of our parents and siblings also.

I am the second oldest of seven children. I was raised as a "parentified" child; both my parents worked two jobs and my assignment was to care for my younger brothers and sisters. I did not have a "normal" childhood filled with camp, vacations, extracurricular activities, parties, and dances. My job was childcare, housekeeping, and excellence in school. My parents constantly reminded me that I was to be a "credit to my race," that "education is the way out of poverty," that "Colored people are as good as White people," and that "you can be anything you want to be." It seemed that the focus for my life was to be a fully productive member of society. I had to jump from childhood to adulthood by fourth grade. Perhaps that is why I seem to function as a natural caretaker and why my friends say that I am afraid to let others take care of me. I know that old habits die hard, but I am working on burying them.

My sisters accepted my role in ministry first. My sister Richelle was living in Denver when I entered ministry and assisted with childcare and typing research papers. She is active in ministry to youth and has a working knowledge of church leadership issues. It helps if one has someone inside the institution to provide a reality check. My other sisters, Miriam and

LaWanda, are my listening safety net. Both have been active laywomen in the church, one in the music department and one as a minister's spouse. I can vent or laugh with them about some of the hassles of motherhood, family, and church politics. They help keep me grounded and give honest counsel. They also remind me that I was once a laywoman. For women in ministry must not lose the connection with women in the congregation, who, for their parts, can be both tireless encouragers and most vocal detractors.

My older brother, William, still treats me like his little sister. He is the only person I could think to call when I was burned out from counseling after the September 11, 2001, attacks. I knew that all of my friends in ministry were also at their limit. He said what I needed to hear just before I imploded. It is a misconception that ministry means we are exempt from fear and confusion. In our humanness we have weaknesses. With all our talk about faith, we need someone else to talk with us too. My brother Kenneth is a distant supporter. Generally, our conversation is around mutual family concerns or my latest work. Leonard, my baby brother, calls me "the Reverend." It is a term of endearment and respect. As his oldest sister I fill the same role I would were I not a minister.

Early in my ministry my family had stereotypical expectations of me as a minister. I am sure it was difficult for many of them. After all, they had known me in some cases for thirty-two years, and I am the first minister in our immediate family. Initially, at family reunions and holidays there was an abrupt suspension of jokes, the hiding of alcohol or snuffing of cigarettes, or an apology for cursing when I entered a room. There were assumptions that I was always ready to pray. Over the years we have settled into a "Yes, Teresa is a preacher and she is still our sister" connection. I have been in conversations with reverend sisters who demand that their siblings comply unquestioningly with their beliefs. I have had conversations with reverend sisters who never interpose any talk of religion with their siblings. I do not know which is best because I do not walk in their pumps.

All of my siblings were baptized as children. We each at some point in our lives have been active in the church. Our conversations do not include obvious God talk but rather adherence to the values taught by our parents and grandparents. Yes, I pray with them. Yes, at times I am a counselor to them. After all, I was their big sister counselor before I ever entered ministry. I do not harp on them about going to church, nor do they rebuke me for my decisions. We are all adults. Their biggest concern is that no one take advantage of me. My brothers do not have a great opinion of contemporary churches yet encourage their children to attend. I have learned when to remove myself from gatherings so I am not an impediment. I ask others to pray at dinners. I refer family and friends to other ministers when I know I cannot go any further with a situation. I try to avoid making myself a stumbling block to their Christian growth and development. It is important to agree to respect their faith development and not expect them to be like me.

It is also refreshing to have a sibling, parent, or grandparent minister to me just as I am.

Eleven years ago my maternal grandfather died after a long battle with lung cancer. Daddy Lyman was one of my most stalwart supports in ministry. A lifelong Baptist layman, he unwaveringly fought for my right to be a minister, even undertaking an eight-hour drive to hear me preach five days after he'd had a chemotherapy treatment. I had a longstanding preaching engagement the weekend he died. I called my grandmother to check the funeral arrangements. I planned to call the host pastor to cancel my participation as preacher for the four-night revival. My grandmother asked me the dates of the revival. I was stunned when she said, "Daddy remembered you said you had to preach. He said for you to go ahead and preach. I am supposed to arrange the funeral for when you can get here." I was not the eulogist because the funeral was to be at the church where he served as treasurer for almost fifty years. I was not allowed to sit in the pulpit but was asked by my family to give remarks. One of the mysteries of God is how we may feel, sense, or intuit the presence of ministering angels or spirits when we are at our weakest moment. I felt like I was going to fall on my face, lose my voice, or dissolve into inconsolable sobs. So I imagined my grandfather sitting in his regular seat smiling, humming, "amen"-ing, and shaking his head as he'd always done. I looked into the faces of my grandmother, uncles, aunts, siblings, and cousins, and I found my voice. I was able to stave off the inevitable until I took my assigned seat, then I allowed my tears to drench my husband's shoulder. Sometimes our safety nets are invisible.

There is no monolithic configuration of women in ministry or their personal relationships. Women in ministry are single, married, separated, divorced, widowed, heterosexual, and lesbian. I had been married to my first husband for about two years when I entered ministry. There were charges and jokes from my husband's friends and men at the church that I picked up the phone when God was calling him. My husband was already in the ordination process and, as far as they were concerned, that was enough. They baited him by asking what kind of man he was to "allow" his wife to do something men do. My mother-in-law was not happy either, saying that my child would suffer since I already spent too much time at church in the choir or teaching. After a few months the marriage disintegrated and I filed for divorce. For about a year after our divorce, whenever my ex-husband entered the sanctuary with his new girlfriend it was like something out of Star Wars—the service seemingly suspended as stares ricocheted from him to me and back, and murmurs subsided only after he sat down. The senior pastor repeatedly asked me if I had considered what would happen to my family when I entered ministry as if I shouldered full responsibility for the divorce. There were congregants who questioned my ability to counsel couples since I was officially single. They apparently felt I had poor judgment about marriage matters since I was divorced. The senior pastor and two other men on staff had been divorced and remarried, so apparently that same standard did not apply to men. I was relegated to the Singles Ministry for a while.

Yes, when women answer the call they typically experience some disruption. I call it our pruning process. God mercifully removes that person or those persons from our lives who would otherwise eventually impede our ministry. I was not happy about the divorce. I felt like a failure. How could I be successful in ministry if I could not keep my home together? I now praise God that I paid attention to directions. I vowed that I would not let another man into my life until my daughter was grown. Ministry was just too hard. The whole relationship thing was not worth the trouble.

After a while I began dating a minister I met at seminary and only our senior pastors were informed of the relationship. His wish that I leave ministry marked the end of our brief relationship. Men asked to go on dates for a variety of astounding and curious reasons. One said he'd always wanted to know what it would be like to kiss a preacher. He obviously had his own problems. Another wanted to help me "become a woman again." Yet another wanted to "investigate what was really under my robe." Because I rebuffed invitations for dates from some of the men in the church and ministers in my conference, an assessment of my sexuality began in earnest. Some said the ulterior motive for my "call" and subsequent divorce was to enable me to have sex with the senior pastor. Women in ministry, as my mother would say, are damned if we do and damned if we don't. I learned the hard way that you cannot argue against a rumor or stop innuendo. The more I tried to deflect the questions about dating, the more warped the suppositions that arose. I empathize with anyone who has ever had to keep her or his personal life under the radar. There were even two women from the church who made it their life's work to cruise through my apartment parking lot, check the cars to see who was at my house, reporting back to their comrades my supposed sexual encounters. I am to this day not sure why it is so important for people to know someone else's intimate secrets.

Small wonder, then, that I did not trust men so much as to help me across the street. I decided just to be married to my ministry and raise my child. I felt depressed just thinking about getting dressed, driving to the church, and entering the parking lot. I was in no hurry to have my life dissected. It was as if my privacy became ancient history when I entered ministry. There was one exception: the parents of two sisters with whom I sang in a gospel group understood the fishbowl effect of ministry. Val and Mahlon provided a space for me to relax and talk about life. Their home became my sanctuary, the place I could laugh, dance, sing, eat, celebrate, play, cry, meet people, and love as a normal human being. They listened, advised, and protected me at church and in the community. Because they sacrificially provided a "safe house" or safety net of sorts, my ministry during the most formative years was enhanced.

Another safety net appeared unexpectedly when I was looking the other way. My friends told me that someone was interested in me. But I had other plans. I planned to finish my doctoral studies, find a job, and live out my life as a credentialed professional and single mother. God's plans were different. Frank removed my stumbling block of thinking that successful women in ministry have to be single or no one wants to be with us because of our dedication to ministry. Now, this brother had to work overtime to convince me that he was not like some of the others. I instantly acquired two adult children, Carin and Kystopher, and now five grandsons, Kevin, Kory, Kile, Kalon, and Kamari, and one great grandaughter, Kamora, with the marriage. Carin and Kystopher had to deal with having a stepmother who happened to be in ministry. It has not been smooth sailing for the same reasons remarriage and blending families would be problematic for women who were not in ministry. I am never sure what this extended family thinks about women in ministry. Kevin, the oldest grandson, lived with us for about two years and accepted ministry as Granny T's job. He occasionally asked questions about my travel and a religion class he took at Clark Atlanta University, and from time to time would ask theological questions, but that was the extent of it. Like most people in the same position, we spent most of the time simply trying to negotiate the fragile stepfamily structure. Blended families and stepfamilies can become stumbling blocks if we let them. Deep spirit work is required to help them desire to become safety nets.

I am not an easy person to live with, especially when I am locked away preparing sermons or lectures, or writing books. I am focused only on the task before me. So God provided me with a husband who can withstand the criticism of allegedly not being a man because he is married to a minister. In fact, often people assume that he is the preacher. I recall once arriving at a church with Frank, and he was the one escorted to the pastor's office while I was asked to sit in the back of the sanctuary. The greeter did not want to hear that I in fact was the Women's Day preacher. She evidently had not looked at the bulletin, which had my photograph prominently displayed. She completely ignored my voice and talked only to my husband. Yes, my husband was carrying my robe but she would not listen. All she saw was someone she thought looked like a (male) preacher. So Frank went as expected to the pastor's office—to tell him *I* had arrived. Soon after, the pastor rushed into the sanctuary where I was quietly reading over my sermon and apologetically swept me up from the bench. The woman greeter stood dumbfounded but said nothing as I walked past.

My husband is my manager. I trust him to make all the arrangements for my preaching and teaching engagements. He also ensures that I do not overbook myself and that no one takes advantage of me. He travels with me often. He avoids sitting in the front row with the minister's spouse. He cooks my favorite foods when I have a preaching engagement, am writing, or have re-turned from a long trip. No, he is not the "wife" reverend sisters joke about needing. He is not perfect but he does support every-thing I do. He also provides honest and critical assessment of my public presentations. Our relationship is not perfect and it is not traditional. We encounter the same stresses of all couples and can-not always pray them away. We work hard at our relationship.

The bottom line is that women can be married, mothers, *and* ministers. But to do so successfully, we have to circumvent the hype and let God work.

Congregants and other ministers also can be stumbling blocks or safety nets depending on their theology, personal faith journey, peer pressure, action of the leadership, and prior asso-ciation with women in ministry. The arguments against women in ministry are legion. People may quote scripture to defer our acceptance. Years of sermons and Bible studies about "bad women" are not easily eradicated. Stories of screaming women evangelists, holier-than-thou women draped in black, or physi-cally weak-voiced speakers may be reiterated by the church leadership. Charges that women with children cannot lead churches or refuse to be itinerants are rampant. Experience is truly the best teacher and unfortunately we are the only ones who can teach people about who we are and what we do. Bishops, district superintendents, regional ministers, elders, and senior pastors may perpetuate the myths that women can-not be ministers or as keepers of denominational polity may see no loopholes for allowing women into ministry. In one-on-one conversations, my brothers in ministry regale me with examples of "women who have not done the work." In lengthier conver-sation, we share examples of women who have done the work.

A number of men have come to accept women in ministry through both personal experience and the moving of the Spirit of God. Those with no prior engagement with women in min-istry may initially be at a loss about what to do. Faced with the prospect of the six female associate ministers being more faithful about their assigned duties than the five male associate ministers, my senior pastor once proclaimed, "I don't know why God gave me all you women. But you at least do the work. I'll just have to do the best I can to teach you." He worked through his dismay by expecting excellence from the women and accepting mediocrity from the men. Male colleagues tell me that their acceptance of women in ministry stems from a multiplicity of reasons. Some never knew of a time women were not in ministry. A number had women as their first religion teacher and spiritual mother. Other said they had been opposed to women being in ministry until they attended seminary and recognized the high standards most women maintain. Many are in the process of trying to turn off old tapes and live in their own experience. Regardless of how the men arrived at acceptance of women, I count men among my most ardent supporters today. Not only do they extend invitations to preach or teach, they also contact me to catch up on our mutual work.

It is not always easy to predict whether someone is likely to become a stumbling block or a safety net. There will be times when people silently press money into your hand or purchase a stole so you can "look more like the other ministers" or suggest a book to build your library and other times when they rally by petition to remove you from an office or blindside you in a meeting. There will be times when they frown the entire time you are preaching and other times when they cannot stop saying amen. There will be times when they proudly proclaim you as their pastor and other times when they act as if they do not care if your draw another breath. There will be months when you are supported in every ministry assigned and other months when the leadership does not invite you to do anything. Sometimes support is reluctant. Sometimes it is nonexistent. Sometimes our work proves our presence. Sometimes it is present from the beginning; we just can't see it.

My experience with women in ministry exemplifies these dichotomies. I entered ministry expecting my sisters to welcome me with open arms. I knew they could teach me the ropes because they had already jumped them. To my utter horror there were women who rejected my presence because I was divorced, had a child, was in seminary, was at a big church, had the protection of a well-known senior pastor, dressed colorfully, rocked heels, talked White, and sang. To my utter delight there were also women who were happy to see me join the ranks precisely because I was divorced, had a child, was in seminary, was at a big church, had the protection of a well-known senior pastor, dressed colorfully, rocked heels, talked White, and sang. I never knew which group would show up when I was at a church, conference, or school. My foremothers used to say that not everyone who says he or she is your friend really is.

There were men and women who pretended to be my friends as long as I agreed with everything they said or did. I had to learn the hard way that there is a difference between ministerial friends and ministerial associates. There were a few brothers who said they would support my ministry only if I would sleep with them. I always refused. God did not say that was part of the call. An older brother in ministry had provided fatherly advice after my divorce. I trusted him and counted him as a friend. One day he propositioned me, saying he wanted to take my sadness away. I thought he was playing. He was not. When I laughed, he promised to make my life a living hell by starting rumors about my sexuality. I was afraid at first that my ministry would be irreparably damaged. One of my play brothers (fictive kin) asked me about the encounter. I told him almost verbatim. He said the man had a reputation in the conference for trying to use his power to seduce or in this case harass women. He suggested I talk to the man's wife. I was hesitant at first but this friend had grown up in the conference and knew everyone and I trusted him. When I saw the wife a couple of days later I told her what had happened. She apologized and said she would handle it. I do not know what the sister said but her husband never bothered me again.

Did you ever meet someone who you knew had your best interests at heart? You know, they always spoke positively to you and about you. They went out of their way to include you in events. They recommended you for preaching or teaching opportunities. Sometimes those we perceive as safety nets in reality are stumbling blocks. They personify the biblical wolves who dress up like sheep to catch you off guard and devour you.

One of my ministry supervisors wrote the book on this behavior. He was one of the most affirming voices during meetings with my ordination boards. I had preached a revival for him and knew his family. He recommended me for a preaching engagement about six hours from home. I told my senior pastor where I was going and received his blessings. I arranged for my daughter to stay with my sister and hit the road. The first four nights of the revival went well. I was scheduled to preach the closing on Sunday morning. The host pastor told me he had received a call from the supervisor informing him that he had decided to preach on Sunday instead of me. I had been preaching for four days so he asked if I minded. I was tired, had a long drive home, and, after all, an elder was arriving. In my denomination deacons and licentiates, at least when I was in the ordination process, are to relinquish assignments or seating in pulpits whenever someone with a higher ordination is present. He missed his flight, so I preached the closing. He arrived in time for the fellowship dinner. He kept looking at me during the dinner but I thought he was being friendly. After dinner he asked to speak to me in another part of the church. To my utter disgust he said that I had to pay him back for the recommendation. My friend Rosetta tells me all the time that I am too logical. I first thought he simply wanted part of the honorarium the host pastor had gone to count. So I'm standing there like Boo Boo the Fool calculating in my head how much I should give him. He said he did not care but I wasn't leaving without fulfilling his price. Then he dropped the other shoe. He threatened to work to have my ordination rescinded if I did not comply with his wishes. I shoved him out of my space just as the host pastor entered the room. He asked what the problem was and the supervisor joked around about being tired and losing his balance. I had not been ordained an elder yet so I was uncertain of institutional protections. I rushed to my car and made my way home. I flew to New York the next day for a fellowship interview.

Still bothered by the confrontation, I requested a dinner meeting with one of my sister elders. I recounted what had occurred. I told her I did not know what effect the denial of his request would have on my ordination process but I would rather leave the church than have to fight the entire time. She gave an exasperated groan and enumerated all the women who had faced similar sexual harassment and assault. She knew the numbers of women who had left the church believing they had no other recourse. She then assured me that that pastor had no power over my life. She confirmed what I already knew but it was good to hear to it from a sister's mouth: she had been where I was trying to go. She advised me to talk to my senior pastor as soon as I returned home. If he did not rectify the issue, I was to call the bishop and speak only to him.

As soon as I returned home, I sped to the church. As I told my senior pastor what happened, he began to yell that he did not know what the man was thinking but that he would not have that thought again. He said he would take care of everything. We prayed and he asked me to leave. He was calling the bishop when I left. The supervisor kept a professional distance the rest of my time in the process. Years later he apologized. My senior pastor was in his own way a father protector. We did not always agree, and in fact frequently engaged in passionate disputes about politics, social issues, or religion, but I respected him as my elder and as my friend. Over the years he would intercede many times for me in matters of this nature. I did not run to him whining, but for support. I am in no way a shrinking violet. There is something in me, however, that slows down my response time when it comes to verbalized sexual threats. Once I am in gear I can handle things. Somehow my pastor always seemed to find out what was going on and had to add his two cents. I generally found out after the fact when he talked to someone. He never mentioned what he had said even when I thanked him. The instances of betrayal or discovery of the ulterior motives in these two examples diminished my trust level in men in ministry.

My good relationship with this senior pastor of mine helped me avoid stereotyping all male ministers as sexual predators. I develop friendships with male ministers as individuals, not lumping them all into the same category. I likewise expect people to get to know me as Teresa and not as women in general.

The situations I've recounted here had positive outcomes. I realize that there are innumerable reverend sisters who do not have senior pastors, male ministers, or elder (more experienced) reverend sister protection. Too many are accosted by people whose ulterior motives become impediments rather than augmentations.

Sadly there are women in ministry who substitute trust with betrayal. One minister whom I had known about six years showed up at my wedding just to tell me the only reason she came was that she knew that my marriage would not last. She said she just wanted to see my face when she told me. I had supported her through several illnesses and charges of misconduct. Her announcement was her wedding gift to me. In her mind women in ministry were not supposed to be married because they were all lesbians. This was her routine critique of any of our friends and acquaintances who dated or had recently married. I realized I was one of her colleagues of convenience, and had never really been her friend. I was supposed to keep her secrets and be available when she was in trouble. She only called when she needed something.

The call to ministry reinforces the mandate for us to be forgiving. People who knew me back in those days knew that I would help anyone. My family taught me to aid sacrificially anyone in need. It was that whole "Vacation Bible School, macaroni glitter covered cigar boxes, popsicle stick model churches, melted ice cream cone, memorized speeches, love the world in spite of" thing. I try to love everyone but I do not suffer fools well. I wanted to rip out this woman's throat. I was ready to take off my head piece, come out of my heels, and throw her down like I had done to William Campbell when I was twelve. This boy who lived up the street tried to run over me with his bike. I stood still as he approached then I flipped him off his bike as he swerved at the last second to avoid me. He was laughing until he hit the ground. He cut his lip when he hit the pavement. I cut my hand. He never tried that again.

I told you I was a fighter. I rarely curse in public but if we had not been in my grandparents' home church around all the people who knew me from birth it would have been on. I was not going to let what my mother would call her "unmitigated gall" ruin my wedding day. I wanted her to leave on her own accord or I was ready to help her trip the light fantastic down the stone stairs.

It was a "Hold me back, girl" moment. You know, one of those times when all you can see is the red around the outline of your target? Everything else is hazy or like a dream sequence. You can't hear anything but the rush of blood in your head. In your "I am not taking this mess any more" mind a little voice prays that someone or something stops you before you wind up wearing some baggy beige or orange jump suit making license plates and sleeping with one eye open all night. Fortunately, my friend Marcia had experience with this type of situation. Observing the contortions on my face she materialized at my side. She leaned over and gave me some Sistah Sense. She reminded me of where I was, and said to think about the insignificance of the person in the full scope of my life. I took a deep breath, forced a smile, thanked the woman for coming, and walked away to greet other guests. Marcia helped me regain my Sistah Sense and, as the mothers in the faith say, I did not let the devil have a place in my life. To be honest with you, my stomach got a little queasy right then just recounting that day for you.

Some affronts linger longer than we think. Months after the wedding I found out the other woman had transferred to another state. I thought of how sad she must have been to go to all the expense of traveling from a beautiful vacation spot some thousand miles away just to signify about my choice of a mate when she could have saved us both time and sent an e-mail. In my "I have to save the world mode" I tried to overlook her obvious need to control. I have released her as a friend. I have seen her once in eleven years and now just have pity for her. I was taught that if you are taken advantage of once it is the other person's fault but if you repeat the same mistake you are to blame. I am a quick study.

The R & B group the O'Jays intoned warnings about smiling backstabbers that I should have taken to heart as I reflect on people from whom I am now estranged. Some of them could not deal with my schedule or my need to turn down certain compromising engagements. Their response was, "You used to be fun; now you just so holy." In retrospect, I understand that their level of discomfort emanated more from comparing themselves to the person they thought ministers should be rather than from something I had actually said or done. I was neither Joan of Arc nor some fire and brimstone "Praise the Lord" fanatic. At one time I made up excuses or really had to work but now I just tactfully decline. If a lay person invites me to a party, I may go for about a half hour, then leave so I do not put a damper on the celebration. Our relationship with laity is an interesting balancing act of common sense and confidentiality.

There was a young man who was hospitalized in an isolation ward. He had been diagnosed with advanced HIV/AIDS, but only the senior pastor, a few of his closest friends, and I knew all the information. As usual the church rumor mill cranked up. (It would be refreshing if the members of church rumor mill would talk about God with the swiftness they dig up dirt.) I began receiving calls asking about him and information about "what they had heard." I, of course, deflected their questions and asked them to pray for him. A woman I had known before I entered ministry called and demanded the "real" information because she had heard you could contract AIDS by breathing the same air as the infected person. (Admittedly, this was early on in the AIDS crisis.) I did not give her the information she wanted. I explained that as a minister I had an obligation to hold his diagnosis in confidence. She said a few unpleasant things, like I owed her since we were supposed to be girls. I said I would do the same for her but we were still girls and could talk about other things. She chose to hang up and did not talk to me for months. After the young man died she came and apologized. She had investigated through other channels (mainly the church rumor mill) and received the information she needed. I was never sure if she understood ministerial confidentiality but we became estranged or different types of friends after that.

Every now and then stumbling blocks are transformed into safety nets. The change may be gradual or cataclysmic. The modification may emanate from something we have said, like a sermon, or something we have done, like visitation to a sick congregant who appreciates the act of ministry. Miss Elsie exhibited such a transformation. An influential lay leader and head stewardess when I entered ministry, she would fold her arms and turn her head whenever I participated in service. She walked by grimacing and never returned my greetings. For a period of time she critiqued everything I did, how I dressed, what I ate, what I said; everything but the air I breathed was wrong in her eyes.

One day I was standing at the front counter in the reception area working on a membership file. She came up and asked me why I looked so sad. I told her about one of the repercussions of my divorce, bills my ex-husband refused to pay. My check was being garnished and I did not know how I was going to pay my rent. For the next hour she told me about the five husbands she had had and how to live through divorce, death, and single parenthood. At the end of our conversation she told me not to worry about anything. She and her stewardess friends had begun to half-way like me. She said I could learn a lot from her. I was instructed to never let her see me cry over a man again. Our newly found common experience superseded her original disdain. I learned that her son was a minister and, because of that, she had long been a stalwart supporter of male pastors. Through our connection she became an unfailing advocate for women in ministry. She determined women were better prepared and more grounded in human nature. She eventually convinced the other stewardesses to give me a chance. In my head, on that day she moved from dragon lady to earth mother. She began to call me daughter and interceded for me until her death.

Peer pressure is an interesting phenomenon. It can help you scale the highest mountain or cause you to crash and burn. A few years ago I was coteaching a class on transformative ministries with a pastor I worked with off and on for about eight years. I had taught his younger sister in Sunday school and in a youth choir when I worked at a Baptist church and was close to his family. He had no biases about women in ministry. Bob and I worked out our lecture schedule and the course requirements and teaching based on our experience levels. The students were an ecumenical gathering of clergy and laity from around Denver. They had enrolled in the ten-week certificate-based night class with the knowledge that a male-female clergy team would be instructing. The first night a small group of Baptist ministers said that they were eager to hear from Bob but that "no woman could teach them anything." I ignored their comments and kept teaching. During question and answer periods they pointedly referenced Bob's information and comments and acted as if I were part of the furniture.

During the fourth week of the class I was asked to preach my first revival. Bob and I decided this provided the perfect opportunity to discuss social change and sexism in ministry. We required the class to attend and instructed them to be ready to evaluate the service in light of our class readings and their personal beliefs. Grudgingly all of them showed up the second night of the revival. Well, as one of my reverend sisters says, it was a case of "nobody but the Lord." One of my most vocal critics was stunned. The next week in class he said that during the revival God spoke to him, and for the first time in his life he understood that women could preach. He said he wasn't sure about all women but he had to accept me as teacher and preacher. He later nominated and successfully campaigned for me to become the first women to preach an ecumenical Black church Thanksgiving service in Denver. He was ridiculed by some of his Baptist colleagues, but said he had to follow the lead of the Holy Spirit and work for gender equality in ministry.

There is an old saying that "when a friend asks there is no tomorrow." During my second year of marriage, my husband, Frank, was diagnosed with severe arterial blockage. He was scheduled for quadruple bypass surgery three days after the diagnosis. I had few friends in Georgia. I felt the burden of facing the surgery with only my daughter and my relatively new sisters-in-law. After I had contacted his family, I began calling my closest reverend sisters for prayer and moral support. Marie and Rosetta were at the hospital within the hour. They are a couple of my older reverend sisters. They have life experience, Mother Wit, and Sistah Sense. These sisters are passionate about praying. I was taught not to let just anybody pray for you. When I need prayer and I want to make sure the prayer gets through to God I call one of them. I trust them with my spiritual life. They reinforce me until I know "God's got this." They even prayed over the surgeon's hands prior to surgery. My husband's cardiologist said that he had never had a family offer to pray for him in person and he knew Frank would be alright with such powerful women in his corner. These sisters set up their own personal "hold my mule" prayer chapel in one of the family waiting rooms. We laughed, told stories, prayed, and sang. I do not remember if we were too loud or the energy just floated through the halls but over the course of those six surgery hours other chaplains, doctors, nurses, and families of other cardiac patients stopped in to request prayer. Marie and Rosetta held forth all day buying food, easing my fears, checking on family, running errands, and fielding phone calls. Other ministers came and went but these sisters were there for the duration. After Frank entered recovery, I had to insist that they go home and rest.

Kim, another reverend sister and lawyer, was in court when I called her. She flew down the morning of the surgery to help me understand living wills and do not resuscitate orders. She returned to New York that evening in order to be in court the next day. She called every day to monitor Frank's progress. My secretary, Dorcas, handled coverage of my classes, notified the faculty, fielded insurance information, and brought me special dinners while I spent the nights on a hide-a-bed next to my husband. Frank's birth sisters stayed for a week watching my daughter and keeping the house together. Frank came home four days before Thanksgiving. My friend Marcia flew in from Denver and fixed dinner so I could rest. Each sister was a real friend. Each filled a particular void without my asking. They sensed exactly what I needed when I needed it. To this day these women are my safety nets.

One of my early lessons in friendships was that one would only have a handful of real friends and incalculable associates. Our real friends may be blood relatives or fictive kin (like non-blood-related so-called sisters and brothers) or people with whom we have an ongoing professional or social relationship. One of my dreams in college was to be a member of a Black sorority. I was the oldest of four girls, so I understood being a big sister, but that new sense of the word "sisterhood" was intoxicating. Yes, there were going to be parties, step shows, service projects, and paraphernalia, but the idea of having a large variety of "sisters" caring for and about each other is what hooked me. I was rushed but was unable to pledge while in college due to finances and a threat by the central administration to lift my Dean's List scholarship because they determined that Black sororities were an academic distraction. Twenty-four years later I became a graduate member of Delta Sigma Theta Sorority. At last I had a group of sisters who shared the same social transformation and academic interests as mine. I have discovered that my sorority membership can be a stumbling block and a safety net in ministry. Black sororities greet their sorors, especially those making public presentations or holding particular offices, with a formal presentation of flowers or small gifts. It is a wonderful practice to honor a sister who they feel exemplifies the sorority's goals and objectives. Sometimes the other sisters in the congregation stand or are in similar attire. This becomes problematic when members of one of the other sororities feel slighted. I have been at churches where I have received mild boos, applause, and animated head shakes when my affiliation is mentioned. I have had women say, "That was alright but the church is not the place for that political stuff," "You were good but you chose the wrong group," or "I enjoyed you but I wish they had invited a _____ (whatever her sorority was)." I have requested that my membership not be mentioned in introductions so women listen without sorority biases. I do not want my personal choices to become stumbling blocks to their spiritual development.

Nonetheless, for me, the security and enhancement aspects of being a sorority member are numerous. I have a built-in support system when I go to a city where I know no one. The connective aspect of sorority life almost ensures that someone in the congregation is my sister. I no doubt have received invitations to preach because a committee chair or spouse is a member of my sorority. When met with negative responses, I say we are all sisters, we just live in different rooms in the same house. Impede my progress or enhance my journey; we are all family.

When I think of stumbling blocks and safety nets I cannot help but remember my best friend, Carrie. I met her in 1975 when I began teaching at Central Missouri State University (now Central Missouri University) in Warrensburg, Missouri. She is a retired university professor and administrator. Carrie is not in ordained ministry but has a ministry of presence and has volunteered as a mentor with countless youth education projects, social service projects, and church administration programs in and around Kansas City, Missouri, for as long as I can remember. Early in our teaching careers when I became aware of the social, racial, and political implications of being one of three Black professors at the school, all in addition to my own personal relationship traumas and the incessant small Baptist church disruptions, Carrie dispensed Mother Wit and Sistah Sense whenever we slowed down enough to share a meal. My rallying cry became her S.O.S. (Signing or Sleeping) paradigm: unless a person signs your check or snores in your face, they have no input in your life. I added "or take care of you when you are sick" (S.O.S.O.S.). I find myself sharing these bits of wisdom in a number of settings. One such was the Candler Women in Theology and Ministry Graduation Banquet in 2002. These excerpts from my speech, entitled "Real Friends," are about coveted support systems.

REAL FRIENDS

The truth of the matter is that real friends are ordinary people
who meet, develop attachments, live, and learn to love
beyond the superficialities of society.
Real friends never get caught up in the trivialities of the
church.
They have no interest in

- who is dating whom,
- who was closest to what professor or pastor,
- who is ordained,
- who will get what sized church,
- who is jealous of whom,

- who sits where and for how long,
- who is what shade on the color spectrum,
- who wears what hairstyle or pierces what body part.

Yes, there will always be alliances based on race, religion, church membership, classes, course structure, small groups, study groups, and political interests.

But God has a way of cross-matching humanity in new relationships that endure even the fierce trauma and drama of seminary education, professional ministry competitiveness, and life's surprises.

God often places together people who in their wildest imaginations would never become close to each other.

Real friends see past difference and look into the heart of a friend.

Real friends walk the same path at times and varied paths at other times yet still learn to love each other for who that other is or is becoming, and then validate the choices each makes.

Real friends grow up together over time, not strangling each other but giving each the room to breathe and blossom.

They do not rush into a relationship as fools do but come to value the Christ in each other.

They see only possibilities in each other, regardless of the time it takes to press toward the mark.

The relationship becomes like fine wine, better with age, which must be sipped and not gulped to be fully appreciated.

Real friends learn to look beyond faults and see needs.

Those extra pounds we need to lose do not turn away our friend but stimulate a concern for our health and encouragement to care for self.

That obnoxious, snorting, spin-around-high-five, fall-on-the-floor laugh we have that can wake up the dead leads our friend to a slow smile or getting the joke before anyone else does.

That situation we get into that would send others running,
gossiping, and pointing a finger spurs our friend into an
immediate problem-solving mode without time or thought
of embarrassment.

When we ran out of money two weeks short of the check, our
friend supplied food and gas money not knowing where
she would get money but knowing we needed help. She
never brought it up again.

When our spouse, friend, parent, or child was sick and we
couldn't make it home, she sat up with us and prayed us
through until the tears stopped and we could sleep.

There were times when we went to the mailbox and there sat
a card or small token just to say "I love you" in celebration
of a small victory or solidarity in a small defeat.

There was that time we were sick and even though our friend
could not stand the sight of any fluid emitted from the
body, she cleaned us, made us soup, got our medicine,
and made sure we were comfortable. . . .

Do you have a real friend?

Are you a real friend?

Remember: When a friend asks, there is no tomorrow.

Whether we are clergy or laity, each of us needs to inventory
our friends, colleagues, and associates to determine who
is a real friend. But we must also inventory the landscape
of our own hearts and minds and see if we are a real
friend to anyone else.

MOTHER WIT AND SISTAH SENSE

Reverend sister girlfriend, listen to what they never tell you in
seminary or the church—Mother Wit and Sistah Sense truisms,
musings, or lessons on stumbling blocks, safety nets, and real
friends:

1. Not everyone who says she or he loves you does.
2. Learn to say not only, "Get away from me, Satan" but also,
   "I don't have time for this right now."

3. Beware of smiling backstabbers.

4. It is difficult to argue people into acceptance. Some things come by the proverbial "prayer and fasting."

5. Cultivate friends who know how to pray for you, not prey on you.

6. Know yourself. Know yourself. Know yourself.

7. Saying "I'm sorry" can be almost as powerful as saying "I love you."

8. Never say, "Never." Life will make a liar out of you.

9. Everyone has something in a trunk or closet no one else need see.

10. You many never meet your greatest supporters face to face.

11. Do not let just anyone or everyone into your house.

12. Choose your friends slowly and wisely.

13. Always check your sources.

14. Sometimes it's good to fly under the radar.

15. Find a safe house and do not tell everyone where it is.

16, Heartfelt hugs heal.

17. God will fight your battles, but stay in shape so you will be ready to fight when God says it's time to engage the enemy.

18. Forgiveness of self and others should expunge the record.

19. You, not your entire family, answered the call.

20. Take time for your family; they are a gift.

21. Allow space for friends and family to minister to you.

22. Divorce is painful but not the end of the world.

23. Men can be as supportive as and sometimes more supportive than some women.

24. Similar biology does mean automatic acceptance.

25. Remember to say thank you.

26. Confidentiality is essential if one is to nurture friendship.

27. Support systems come in all ages, races, ethnicities, religions, health, and economic status.

28. Get out of the way and let God work.

29. Try to avoid letting your personal relationships or social affiliations become stumbling blocks to others.

30. Your life may become unwittingly a source of pride or a symbol of redemption for others.

Women in ministry need spiritual, social, psychological and emotional undergirding as we live this life of service to others. We may have a special call, but we are human beings. Preachers need that proverbial wind beneath their wings too. Those who have real friends are blessed. We cannot be all things to all people because we are not God. We will make mistakes and trust the wrong people for the wrong reasons. We will trust the right people for the right reasons. We may become our own worse stumbling block. The good news is that God gives us discernment if we will pay attention. Sometimes the best safety net is solitude. Whether we encounter stumbling blocks or safety nets, God will give us strength for the journey.

Love, your friend,
Teresa

FIVE

⊡

NO WOMAN
IS AN ISLAND

⊡

Dear Daughters of the Covenant,

Most people find it difficult to believe that am an introvert. I am internally traumatized when I have to make public presentations. I do not sleep well the night before a sermon. I have to encourage myself before each lecture, hospital visit, or conference session. I like to be alone. I can work for hours at a time and not miss human conversation or physical contact. I would rather complete projects myself than depend on others. Part of the predicament is that I have encountered too many people who say they will do something but do not follow through, leaving others to rush around to meet deadlines or correct avoidable mistakes. I try to be a woman of my word. Yes, I occasionally miss the mark. I take responsibility for my slack behavior and try not to leave anyone hanging.

The other component in this need to do for myself is that I am a perfectionist. I have high standards of performance and too often expect others to adhere to them. Unfortunately, perfectionism can lead to fatigue and self-imposed isolation from the very people who can help lessen the load, join the fight, and fill in some of my gaps. I am not advocating mediocrity or always traveling with an entourage. I am suggesting that I comprehend that I can't do everything, be every place, know all the information, have all the right answers, or be by myself all the time. Ministry is a corporate enterprise. Assistance is required for effectiveness. Having someone you trust to help you soar is a blessing. Choosing the right mentor or mentors is a survival skill.

There is an established precedent for women working, traveling, shopping, dining, worshiping, gossiping, protesting, praying, and even giving birth together. Women seem to have a natural sense of affiliation. Mary Magdalene had that group of "certain" women who followed Jesus. Carry Nation had temperance workers. Aimee Semple McPherson had her publicity caravan. Harriet Tubman had the Underground Railroad. Pauli Murray had other civil rights activists. My grandmother had the Missionary Sisterhood. On the contemporary religious scene it seems one is not considered a success unless one has a retinue larger than the children of Israel, a designer-suit, color-coordinated entourage, Bluetooth-synced, product-laden armor bearers, or reciprocal presenters on the "sisters'" conference circuit. I am keenly aware that there are reverend sister bishops, ministers, pastors, evangelists, and prophetesses whose preference is to travel with one or more women whose assignment is to carry her robe or change of clothes, drive the car, provide water or some other liquid concoction, secure her Bible and, when applicable, her manuscript, and sell their DVDs, CDs, or books.

My family members frequently travel with me, intercede on my behalf (particularly if I am exhausted), arrange follow-up engagements, secure the honorarium, or sell my products following services. A few of my reverend sister friends sporadically accompany me as a sign of support for women in ministry in general and me in particular. It is never my expectation that they schlep anything for me. (Remember my independent nature!) They do, however, protect me from myself by driving or giving me the unspoken space or support I need.

As attractive as it may be to have a crowd of supporters, followers, or handlers, the majority of women in ministry do their work solo, in pairs, or in small groups. Although public perception of the efficacy, "anointing," or power of one's ministry is habitually associated with numbers in the seats, esteem of men, or size of the advance team, in fact many women do the work in isolated areas, are the only woman on a staff or without any ministerial colleagues whatsoever, or simply lack support for what they do. Whether one travels alone or in a group, the tasks, complications, vicissitudes, and joys of ministry can deplete one's social, emotional, intellectual, physical, and spiritual energies. If we are not careful, we will give so much of ourselves we will not recognize who we are.

There is no monolithic "woman in ministry." What works for one may not work for another. The absence of a clique or cohorts does not equal an insignificant ministry. When we least expect it, no matter how adept we are at navigating the process, we will need someone to help us make sense of it all.

I keep in mind a Saturday morning women's conference at a small church in Doraville, Georgia, in the later 1990s. I was in the middle of presenting a workshop on women reclaiming their voices when I was distracted by the unsettling entrance of three women dressed in sequined pink suits. As they noisily positioned themselves in the front row I attempted to refocus the group's attention on the presentation. For the remainder of the session they held their own little conversation as if I were not there. As I took my seat after the question and answer period one of the women was introduced as the next speaker. She immediately launched into a critique of my presence. "I did not go to seminary. I don't need no degree to talk about the Lord. I only say what the Spirit gives me." I sat there trying to figure out whether to get up and leave or not. I had just spent two hours telling women to stand up for themselves so I sat there trying to look at her. She was not finished with me yet. "I am here today because my husband said I could come here and minister to you. I'm going you tell you how to find your voice, get his credit card, and go to Victoria's Secret. By the way, I didn't see no one with that woman who was up here. Don't ever listen to a woman who travels alone and calls herself a minister. These ladies here go with me wherever I go to protect my anointing." I sat through the rest of her speech, then excused myself, shook the dust off my feet, and went home.

We had different theologies and views of ministry but she was entitled to her opinion. I do not expect everyone to agree with me but I do not appreciate personal attacks. As soon as I got in my car I hit the cell phone. I was unable to reach the folk I generally talk to when I'm going through this kind of thing but was able to connect with one of my brothers in ministry. I do not know if I ever said "Hello" but he patiently listened while I ranted about sisters not supporting sisters. He did not justify my anger and frustration. He was not judgmental. He did not give the definitive answer. He merely reminded me I was again caught off guard because the perpetrator was a woman. He said he knew I would have had a rebuttal if a man had done the same thing. He was right. Sometimes the reflection in the mirror is painful. Then he asked me what my next move would be, and I left hurt mode and began to plan some seminar on women's relationships or something. My head cleared, my focus returned, and I realized that after that fifteen-minute conversation I was once again ready to move on with my life. I cannot do this ministry thing on my own. I have learned to be selective, however, about who teaches me and leads me.

Ministers are human beings. Ministers, therefore are subject to the same issues as others. We become confused, nonproductive, angry, hurt, aggressive, depressed, and tired. We are comical, verbose, playful, inquisitive, and mischievous. We may step off course for a season. We may work ourselves to death. We do not have all the answers even for ourselves. No matter how many years we have been in ministry, we still don't get it all right. No matter how many people we maintain to care about and for us, we have to answer to God for ourselves. No matter how efficiently we complete tasks, something will fail. No matter how many degrees we earn, we will forget information. No matter how many congregants we pastor, we have to answer to a higher power. No matter how many miles we travel or hours we clock, we need a centering place. Yes, ministry is sacrificial. (Carrying a cross is required. Getting on it is not.) Who ministers to ministers? Whom do we allow a glimpse into our most vulnerable spaces? Who, besides God, knows a fragment of what we are going through? Who cleans up our wounds, applies the proper astringent, and deftly applies bandages after a church battle? Who knows from experience when to act and what to say to encourage us to keep going? Whom do we trust enough to point out our growing edges and our maturing expertise? Whose behavior, proclamation, writings, lifestyle, or faith assists us in living out our calls and remaining essentially in "all things through Christ" mode? Who mentors the mentor?

Mentors, consultants, confidants, coaches, tutors, counselors, teachers, or wise women are individuals, small groups, organizations, or institutions; they are the contents of books, movies, and songs that guide us, teach us, and sustain us. There are no social restrictions on who is able to mentor whom. Mentors possess life experience, expertise, wisdom, or knowledge that may benefit another person's growth and development through noncompetitive interaction. Effective mentors savor their work. Mentors strive for excellence and know their own limitations. Good mentors learn as well as instruct. They teach by precept and example. Mentors know when to speak and when to listen. They establish trust, keep confidences, and provide honest feedback. They encourage rather than demand. Some model through direct physical interaction while others never meet their protégé. Mentors are not perfect. They are not experts in all things. They do not denigrate nor manipulate their students. Mentors are not babysitters. Mentors do not do all the work while the mentees takes it easy. Mentors have to speak the truth in love. Mentors do not always agree with the mentees. Mentors cannot be all things to all people. Mentors know when to take their hands away so you can stand on your own. Mentors know how to stand in the shadows and let you shine. Mentors need mentors too.

Blessed with opportunities to speak and preach worldwide, I meet hundreds and thousands of people each year. Without fail following each engagement I am asked through face-to-face, e-mail, or telephone contact to become someone's mentor. I know that the number of ordained women clergy still pales beside the number of male clergy. I have preached in churches or conferences where I am the first woman to be invited to preach (not speak, but preach), even in the twenty-first century. Women are hungry for someone to tell them they are not hearing voices or need to be committed but confirm that they are responding to a divine invitation. Women are interested in how to retain their femininity in a man's domain. They are passionate about having someone to talk to on a continuing basis. They desire a compassionate, listening, empathetic, and in some cases sympathetic ear. Replies and queries consist of "I want to be like you," "How do you find the power to do what you do?" "I'm thinking of leaving the church; should I?" "I could never do that," "After you leave we will go back to the same old treatment, "There aren't any women I trust enough to talk with about this," "You look like a woman," "We are only allowed to sit up here today because it's Women's Day," or "My pastor said I needed to meet you because I need a female role model." I usually ask what the person means by mentoring, why she asked me, her responsibility in such a relationship, her expectations of my mentoring and time commitment. Some want a mentor during the ordination process. Some desire a listening post while they complete a degree. Some want an ongoing conversation partner regarding family relations. Some request a lifelong support system. Some are seasonal. Some need a "woman's opinion" cn ministry. Some need a "fill in" until their other mentor is available.

While it would be wonderful to mentor each of them, I know that that is a physical, emotional, and spiritual impossibility. We each have limited knowledge and cannot be all things to all people. I would not be honest with myself if I let my ego appoint me as the definitive voice for all women or men in ministry. I can only supply a Teresa Lynn view of the "how to's" of ministry and a miniscule idea of how to live as a Black woman. I realize that I have been blessed with certain talents and gifts and try to use them with integrity. I also recognize that there are those who are infinitely more gifted than I. So I share candidly with each sister or brother that I am unable to provide twenty-four-hour on-call support. The best way to contact me is through e-mails or occasional phone calls. I will help as much as I can. I want to encourage women in ministry and understand that I am not God. I cannot be everywhere. I prefer to do well in a limited context than poorly in a broad context. Frequently, a person may request assistance but I sense that it would be better if someone else works with that person. I try to be forthright about my referral rationale and if requested work with people as they connect with other mentors. I advise them to cultivate mentor relationships closer to home through friendships with others involved in ministry. There are women who are immediately offended that I do not "have enough time for a sister," and who ask "Who do you think you are?" but that is rare. Some sisters are so needy that they seem to drain me emotionally. Some are upset by my relationship with other people. Some develop a combative spirit, deflecting anything I say. These relationships are short lived.

My lifelong mentor is God. God is the source of the inner voice that reaffirms what I have been taught my entire life by the people God provided to insure that I would survive and thrive. This is my primary survival tool. My mentors are the relatives and strangers, Sunday school teachers and academics,

community and religious leaders, the domestics and day laborers, believers and nonbelievers, drunks and druggies, supervisors and colleagues, and the professionals and prostitutes from
childhood forward. They tutored me by relating their life experiences and beliefs, their successes and failures, their joys and
sorrows, their well-honed expertise and their in-process knowledge. Some did not have the proper or sufficient language to
describe what I was to learn but said it anyway. They were willing to share whether I was willing to listen or not. Some were
the first of their generation to achieve a particular goal, yet they
never forgot those who did not make it.

I did not appreciate or use many of their teachings until
years later when I encountered similar experiences. Many of
these people shielded me from the deep pains of life and de-
clared that they never wanted me to go through what they had.
Many used negative lessons to steer me into a better life. They
interpreted interpersonal, communal, national, and global life
through the lens of their own experience and allowed a space
for my own trial and error. They encouraged me when I was
right and gently corrected me when I was wrong. Their intergenerational teaching by precept and example, hands-on instruction and honest acknowledgement of not knowing what to
say presented the consummate model for being a mentor and
seeking a mentor. They demonstrated that the essence of mentoring is a willingness to share, not as experts but as human beings who passed a class. I realize people want a living, breathing, talking mentor. I suggest reading materials or other media
as a stop-gap measure. While there is a plethora of ghost-written, superficial self-help material, there are also some rich resources to assist one on the journey through ministry.

I have several "little brothers" who make sure I am protected when I travel, listen when I am confused, pray for my
ministry, invite me to their churches, and seek counsel for various aspects of their lives. I do not know where I would be in
ministry without sound counsel from some of my brothers in

ministry. They provide a different perspective than my sisters and I believe balance is necessary. There have been male bishops who have allowed me to grow as a teacher in a world that says all ministers are pastors. They tutored me in my quest to be a different kind of minister. They also seek a listening ear from an "outsider" who understands some of the inner workings of institutionalized religious structures. Toxicity in mentoring knows no gender bounds. I have encountered young men who begin with the "I identify more with women than men since my mother raised me" conversation. They voice their need for a balance of male and female mentors. Every now and then one arrives that uses the request for coaching as a smoke screen for ascertaining what women are "up to" and acquiring information to advance themselves.

I have had encounters with young men who have taken materials I shared with them and published them as their own. One even asked me to write the foreword to "his book" on preaching, stating that he appreciated my help but women would not be accepted in his denomination teaching or preaching. Another "son in ministry" seemed to hang on every instruction. I worked diligently to make sure he had opportunities to do ministry. He was bright, articulate, and willing to do anything to become a pastor. Everything—including talking about me behind my back, critiquing my marital status, fomenting rumors about his understanding of my sexuality, demeaning my intelligence, and maneuvering to take my position as chief associate pastor. He eventually left the denomination, started his own church, and thank God over the years moved to a more open and gender-inclusive ministry. Thankfully most men have proven to be great students, colleagues, and friends. They are immensely supportive. I am proud of their accomplishments as scholars and pastors. Gender-inclusive partnerships are critical to our success in ministry.

Sister mentors come in all forms. My twenty-five–year-old daughter has an uncanny ability to recall a "But, Mom, you said" just when my confidence or energy is waning. As I watch her negotiate life using some tools my grandmothers, community mothers, and other mothers passed on to me, I understand the value of Mother Wit and Sistah Sense. Like her, I am mentored by the direct and indirect actions of others. My reverend sister friend Zelia sends text messages to pray for me or give confidence to me when I travel. She is an English teacher, and her speech reminds me the way my foremothers stressed "talking proper will get you farther than that other stuff (teenage vernacular). I don't care how other children are talking. I did not send you to school to be a fool. You will never find a job other than cleaning up for someone else sounding like that." I taught speech pathology and audiology classes, at the beginning of which we had discussions about acceptance of standard or nonstandard English for Black students. I constantly reminded the Black students that Black English was fine at home or with peers but they had to be multilingual in public. I love language and this sister friend Zelia is my language mentor. She serves as an editor by reading manuscripts before I submit them. She listens critically to my sermons and gives sound feedback. She has a wealth of knowledge about literature and indirectly yields a treasure trove of sermon illustrations during our everyday conversations.

Sandra is one of the first reverend sister friends I had in my life. We live on separate coasts and were raised in different cultures. Over the past twenty years she has been my chief ministerial compass, coconspirator, cocommiserator, cocaptain of my cheerleader squad, collegial confidant, and sister confessor. We see each other at annual denominational meetings. Most of our contact is on the telephone or via e-mail. Sandra is the queen of the well-placed word, joke, or bit of information. She is quietly adept at assessing human nature. She is politically astute. Sandra has that older sister way of preventing one from running into the last wall she crashed into or was helped to avoid by one of her mentors. Sandra is a prayer warrior and pastoral counselor. She understands which role she needs to fill at the particular moment.

Marie and Darlene are my bookends. Marie is a slightly older woman in ministry with experience as a senior pastor. She raised five sons as a single parent. Marie helps me negotiate family obligations and church responsibilities. She is the person I call on to pray me through health crises. Darlene is my daughter in ministry and a long-standing friend. Her daughters and my daughter sang in the same children's choir. She is never without a word of encouragement and support. Darlene found time to see the bright side of life even when she was recovering from neurological surgery or caring for a sick family member. Her husband and my husband, both retired, inadvertently model being the spouse of an active woman in ministry. When our schedules allow, Marie, Darlene, and I meet monthly over dinner to talk through ministry madness and majesty, family life, professional goals, and self-care from our particular perspectives. Regardless of the types of characteristics or configurations of these sister mentors, their presence in my life is invaluable. When we come together, sometimes we resolve life, sometimes we rehash concerns, but mostly we take time to be in the company of each other as sisters who help us remember we are women who have been called into ministry.

Other venues for mentoring are lay women's organizations, ministerial alliances, clergy women's support groups or safe spaces, or viable ministry associations. In the 1990s I was privileged to found an organization for lay and clergy women in Denver, Colorado. Sisters Working Encouraging Empowering Together (S.W.E.E.T.) was an intergenerational mentoring and networking program. The women in the group supported my ministry. They nurtured and nourished each other through health care information, child care, career counseling, religious instruction, artistic presentations, and sister care. I realized that clergy women had some other needs so shortly before I left Denver a couple of us began an ecumenical group called Sisters in the Spirit. Our major goal was to provide a safe space for women in ministry to be women. We helped each other with sermons, counseled each other, played games, attended each other's special occasions, and when possible traveled to another sister's engagement as her "amen corner."

Many of you belong to denominational women in ministry groups. I advocate taking advantage of the counsel, tutoring, and mentoring these organizations can supply. Cognizant of the fact that in some places men restrict women's involvement in these groups, I can only say that you need to seek your healing like the woman with the issue of blood: press on in spite of the social limitations. If there is not a denominational body of women, ordained and nonordained, seminary educated and life-experience educated, young and old, or married and single, then start one yourself. Annual attendance at women in ministry and women's ministry conferences is an excellent idea, and each person needs something or someone to sustain them until the next special event. These gatherings are sometimes like a large group therapy. Some healing is better than no healing at all.

Mentoring can get messy. Some people do not want to be healed. Some sisters have not matured enough to either give or accept help. Some thrive in confusion. Some think the sun rises and sets just for them. Some are sponges that continue to soak up the goodness you provide but never give anything back. There are times when role confusion may arise. There will be sisters who will request your consultation, then decide that they need to correct your behavior or beliefs. They will demean everything you do. They will plot to take your place while selling their souls to the highest bidder. They will copy your mannerisms, plagiarize your presentation content, imitate your oral mannerisms, dress in your distinctive style, and purport to speak for you. There once was a teaching assistant who waited until I was at a conference to announce to my class that she may not have my degrees or positions or dress exactly like me but she knew more. According to the tape, she then began to take apart everything I had taught the class to that point. She neither taught for me again nor conversed with me about her needs.

She felt that she needed to be in competition with me because we were both Black women and she wanted to be where I was without crawling over anything I had to endure to get the job.

Such subtle or blatant sister competitiveness rears its ugly head in the strangest manner and place. There was a nontraditional, late thirties, full-grown, owned-house, full-time-job-should-have-known-better woman student who asked me the first week of class to be her mentor. She grew up Baptist and had no female role models in her church. While in seminary she attended a local church pastored by one of my female colleagues. We were about five years apart in age so I thought it would work. I thought there would be little groundwork to do. She shared her goals in ministry and academics. She talked. I listened. She had, as my grandmother would say, good sense. She seemed sane. Things went well for about six months when her pastor called me to say she was draining the life out of her with constant complaining and whining. I called the student for some sister face-time and she said the pastor was confused and didn't like other women in ministry. I met with my sister pastor colleague and she reiterated the emotional and spiritual depletion effected by the student's behavior. I thought I would give the situation some space since I had other counseling commitments. About two weeks later the student showed up at my front door unannounced. I try to keep students and home separated unless there is a specially invited sister gathering. She began talking as soon as I opened the door. "I hate you. It is not fair that you have a house, a child, a husband, and a Ph.D. and I have nothing. Why you? I don't know why people think you are better than me. I do not understand why God has blessed you and not me." First I wanted to retaliate. Then I had to do the proverbial count to ten before I asked her to leave my home. I told her that I did not appreciate her accusations, yet I understood the tremendous boundary issues that were evident. I also realized I could no longer consult with her. I fall back on Carrie's S.O.S. teachings. I said "I am sorry you feel this way but unless you walk in my pumps, do not judge who I am or what I have achieved. I am not your competition. You are. Now please leave my house." At first she refused, then left cursing the air. We had a strained professional relationship until she graduated.

You know what works best for you. Your choice of mentor depends on your personality, social location, motivation, communicative style, management approach, and particularity of your need. Mentoring relationships fall apart or end due to growth of the individual seeking assistance. When class is over everyone goes home or moves to a different class. This does not mean one forgets the mentor; it merely means that the student has become the teacher. There may be too much geographical distance hindering contact between the parties. There are limited opportunities for me to see sisters face to face particularly when I meet them at a conference. If we are not in sustained contact, our attentiveness to a circumstance or discussion of an issue is fragmented at best. Time management or conflicting schedules may interfere with opportunities to give or receive support. I am constantly on the move, working between the seminary and engagements worldwide. I also have a home life. Effective mentoring has to take a number like everyone else. This does not mean I do not care about a person. It means that I have to prioritize. So before you solicit a mentor or act as a mentor, review the God Sense, Mother Wit, or Sistah Sense your life has already provided.

MOTHER WIT AND SISTAH SENSE

Reverend sister girlfriend, listen to what they never tell you in seminary or the church—Mother Wit and Sistah Sense truisms, musings, and lessons on staying connected to the mainland:

1. Learn to listen to *your* inner voice to self-mentor. You have had invaluable but often submerged life experiences that are more instructive than another person could be to you.

2. Know why you need a mentor before you ask.

3. Similarly, examine carefully another's motivation for requesting that you mentor her.

4. Find out as much as possible about a person before you seek to emulate that person.

5. No one is perfect, so learn to use the positive and the negative aspects of someone's personality, life, and ministry.

6. Everyone answers to someone.

7. Building a sound mentoring relationship takes trust and time. Some tutorials take seconds, others take years.

8. Try to keep your mentoring space and home space separate. You need a sanctuary to revive and reconnect with yourself.

9. One may require a different mentor for different areas of one's personal life, vocation, or avocation.

10. Do not kill the messenger. If you trust someone enough to tell you the truth or request that person's support, then listen, evaluate, and finally act.

11. Remember what Mama said: "Not everyone good to you is good for you."

12. Mentoring is about mutuality. It is not about selfish entitlement or an opportunity to abdicate personal responsibility.

13. Not everyone is capable of nor desires to be a mentor.

14. Be cautious around folk who are always volunteering to be your mentors.

15. Build a team you can trust to keep you grounded and let you soar.

16. Mentors are human beings, so allow space for mistakes.

17. Allow others to minister to you. They will be a blessing and you will be blessed.

18. No one has all the answers. If you do not know, do not make something up.

19. The battle belongs to God and you have to be willing to fight when God calls you into service.

20. Do not mistake mentors for persons who will be accessible twenty-four hours per day.

21. Sometimes you are the driver and sometimes you have to ride in the back seat.

22. Trust Sistah Sense particularly when that sister is older, wiser, and healed of her battle scars.

23. Use what you have learned from others to teach someone else.

24. Some people seem to be ordained to sap the life blood out of you. Refer them to a different blood bank. We are not here to save the world. Someone already paid for the transfusion.

25. Jealousy is a green-eyed monster wearing matching pumps.

26. If the relationship seems to radically change, know when to say thank you and end it.

27. Mentors come in all ages, colors, denominations, life experiences, and both genders. Platonic relationships are possible. Variety is the spice of life and the proper seasoning for ministry.

28. Your mentor's success is not a guarantee that you will succeed in the same arena or at the same level.

29. If God had wanted clones, God could have created them. Remember who you are. You are not your mentor. She has to walk in her own pumps and you in yours.

30. Mentoring can become labor intensive. Jesus took sabbaticals. Mentors need them also.

31. Children will remind you of what you really believe.

As I was writing this letter to you, my husband was diagnosed with a rare form of cancer. After the initial shock, awe, and fear subsided, I began to reach out to the people whom I valued as one type of mentor or another. I sat down, prayed, and realized that I could not walk through the crisis by myself. Yes, I called Frank's children and sisters. Yes, I called my family and daughter. I prayed again and was led to call or e-mail friends in ministry, colleagues, close family friends, and my bishop. I did not go into all the aspects of Frank's immediate health concern, but rather asked all these friends to pray. There was a sense of relief as prayers were e-mailed to me or people began to stop by to pray or just chat.

As you have heard me say, I am an introvert and usually operate on behalf of others under the radar. I am not saying that we do things just so people will be with us when we are going through the valley. What I am saying is that we all need someone sometime. I could not help but think how much harder life would be if I were not connected to those who know my needs and are willing to sacrifice to ensure they are supported. No woman is an island. She will drown if she does not have others to buffer some of the waves, lend her a tried and true life raft, send reinforcements when she is under attack, or call on God when she cannot do it for herself. Yes, sisters can be tough, take charge, and handle their business, but even Jesus had some human backups to help spread the Word.

Thank you all,
Teresa Lynn

SIX

CARVING OUT
YOUR OWN SPACE

My Sisters in God's Service,
We know that historically women have held 99 percent of the jobs in the church. The "final frontier," the brick ceiling, the road less traveled, the land of the big chairs, the testosterone zone, and the "for boys only club" has been the senior pastorate. Yes, there are women who serve as the founder, leader, organizer, financier, chief cook, bottle washer, janitor, and sole pastor of churches. Yes, there are women who have large "ministries" developed over years of struggle. Yes, there are women who have been elected or proclaimed bishop in so-called mainline denominations. Yes, there are women who have left the church of their childhood to pursue ministry "under their own vine and fig tree." Yes, there are women who are in search of a place where their call is honored and their work unobstructed.

As a church musician, my mother used to play "May the Work I've Done Speak for Me." The lyrics bring to mind my grandfather's evocation that "all work has dignity." God alone will judge the value of what we do, no matter how small or large our work seems by human measurements. I wonder, given the resistance some of us face, what "labors" or "works" will indicate our faithfulness when we have retired from our appointed ministries? God did not call us to a finished product but one that is under construction. Someone has to draw up the blueprints, another locate the site, another clear the land, another procure building materials, another hire and oversee the crew, another subcontract those with expertise in specific areas, another inspect the product, and yet another test the product. Everyone has a purpose and responsibility. God will not ask us who tried to stop us, hinder us, deny us, or keep us out of the pulpit. God will ask if we did the work.

There will be times when you are ready to do the work. You have all the faith, friends, finances, materials, management, and moxie needed to do an excellent work for God. Without warning you are blindsided by someone who has stayed up late to construct a Sears Tower–size stumbling block in front of you. This person gathers his or her own troops to sabotage and denigrate your every effort. The naysayers seem to outnumber the yes-you-cans. When I contemplated running for the office of director of Christian Education for my denomination, the first surreptitious slanderous naysayer was a woman in ministry who constantly intoned, "You may be a teacher but you are not a real minister." I learned over the course of my short campaign that she was one of the loudest voices against me in private but publicly supported me when the leadership of the church was present. I was shocked initially that a "sister" would play the same game I had experienced countless "brothers" as playing over the years. She had learned the good ol' boys' rules and played her good ol' girls machinations with verve. Sadly, she has not learned that "touching the head of God's anointed" would mean few friends when God's repercussions began to prevail.

Early in my ministry a wonderful family heard of my desire to pastor a church. They proceeded with a demographic study and business plan, secured a building and initiated door-to-door canvassing to determine the feasibility of establishing a church in the southeastern part of Denver where there was no African Methodist Episcopal (A.M.E.) Church but a growing presence of professional African Americans who desired to attend a Black church. As an ordained elder I followed protocol and contacted the proper persons to present the church plant plans. I was excited that I would soon be the pastor of a new church. Well, as soon as some heard of the plans they began seeking a male to lead the church. That year at the conference they appointed a male deacon to plant a new church in the opposite direction. At a conference I was told that it would be better if I stayed at my home church. The rationale was that I would siphon members from the established A.M.E. churches. While about twenty potential members lived in the area selected for the new church led by the male deacon, the other eighty who wished to join were left unaffiliated. The project died and even twenty years later there is not a church of my denomination in that area.

I knew that God had told me to begin the work of building this new church and yet the human authorities did not believe me. I was utterly crushed and had a crisis of faith. I tried to discern if the barriers were due to my gender or their fear of a new church succeeding in an untapped area. I believe with all my soul it was a combination of the two. The biblical text says: "Do your best to present yourself to God as one approved by him, a worker who has no need to be ashamed, rightly explaining that word of truth" (2 Tim. 2:15). I learned to recite it until I believed that all things would work out for my good since I had tried to be obedient to God. I remained at my home church in associate pastor, assistant to the pastor, assistant pastor, and supply pastor positions until I relocated to Atlanta. I have since held positions as assistant pastor and associate pastor and Christian Education director but never as a senior pastor. The good news is that twenty years later two of the churches in the Denver area are pastored by women. Perhaps I was ahead of my time. Only God knows. In any event God always provides a means for us to work out our call. James 2:17 reminds us that faith without works is dead. It is our duty is to remain faithful until we find the soil that God has promised for growth and development.

Over the centuries women called by God have established ministries in places often overlooked. Women of faith have long been doing church work without benefit of acknowledgement, ordination, or community support. Whether they were serving as senior pastors, copastors, evangelists, chaplains, revivalists, conference preachers, or social activists, they did the work of ministry. They have survived (lived above unfavorable circumstances) and thrived (exceeded even their own expectations) through pastoring small mission and "dying" churches, feeding houseless folk and taking in orphans, preaching in supermarkets and on street corners, visiting hospitals and houses of prostitution, traveling in groups and going solo, leaving children and leaving jobs, carrying protest signs and voter registration cards, and walking other women through the pains of childbirth and child loss. Regardless of their titles, they were living out their calls. There are countless other traditional and nontraditional avenues for ministry. There are alternative "pulpits" to the sanctuary with the big chair. Since all ground is sacred, consider what you would add to this list of "holy" places for carving out your own space for ministry:

- Missions, foreign and domestic
- Schools—pubic and private mentoring and tutoring
- Hospitals, clinics, hospice chaplaincy
- College and university campus ministries
- Seminary and Bible college teaching
- Corporations—employee designated volunteer Bible studies and ethics discussions
- Corrections institutions—prisons, reentry or transitional programs

- Government—for example, legislative chaplaincy
- Pastoral care and counseling
- Religious education—summer youth camps and training institutes, adult catechesis
- Art and design—textiles, painting, vestments, iconography
- Sanctuary architecture
- Music—composition, teaching, performance
- Administration and organizational management
- Recreation—youth camps and adult respite care
- Gerontology and senior care centers
- Rural circuits and exurban sprawl centers
- Foster care and adoption
- Social service assistance
- Military chaplaincy
- Mental health work of all kinds
- Retreat or conference development and leadership
- Grief and funeral counseling
- Church financial planning and stewardship seminar leadership
- Rehabilitation center work
- Peace and justice ministry
- Transportation—for example, work at airport chapels and truck stop chapels
- Special interest groups—for example, NASCAR or motorcycle ministries
- Athletics—for example, golf club prayer groups or counseling
- Political institutions and social activism
- Natural/national disaster and relief agencies
- Homeless shelters, domestic violence safe houses, youth detention centers

- Media and sound ministries—television, radio, film, Internet sites, journalism
- Conference or circuit preaching for specific audiences, for example, women in ministry

The list merely scratches the surface of possibilities. The important thing is to assess one's own skills, resources, training, flexibility, and adaptability to multiple contexts of ministry. Attend to the layers of your call, then work with the one or ones most attainable while continuing to develop means for the primary focus of your ministry. This will lessen the anxiety and fatigue of fighting the battle to become God's instrument.

My call to ministry, as I have said before, was and is clearly to teach, preach, and write. At least twice a year since 1983, I have been told that I am not a real minister because I do not pastor a church. It does not seem to matter to these critics that I counsel undergraduate and graduate students and other ministers nationally, yielding a "congregation" in the thousands. It is of no consequence to such detractors that I work on the staff of various churches as a Bible study teacher, ministry organizer, liturgist, or workshop presenter. It is apparently irrelevant that I preach three to ten times per month depending on the itinerant destination and stipulated occasion. It is meaningless to them that through writing about what God has placed within me I am able to reach out globally to untold people in several different printed languages. It is apparently not obvious that I work ecumenically on various conferences to ensure the church universal is served. It is obviously a secret that God has called me to minister through the spoken word. Yet precisely such soul-stirring critique has come from the mouths of men, but more readily from the mouths of women who equate "call" language only with titular leadership of a congregation or "preaching" the Word. This I believe to be a narrow and superficial view of the expanse of ministry and directions from God that individuals receive without others overhearing the details.

There are a number of places for us to carve out our own space for ministry. The primary space for my teaching/education ministry is clearly in the classrooms of my assigned "church office," Bishops Hall at Candler School of Theology at Emory University in Atlanta, Georgia.

As a child of the '50s I was taught that education was a ticket out of despair. I immersed myself in books and took mental trips to every country in the world, developed an appreciation for ancient cultures and a love of language. In my young adult life I was told, "You can't teach what you don't know and you can't lead where you won't go." In church my entire life I have been reminded of the biblical injunction about studying to show oneself approved. Teachers at one time were respected in the Black community. I had never had a Black female professor and there were none on the faculty when I was a student at seminary. The journey of my academic foremothers and their persistence in spreading a "gospel of intelligence" is the foundation of my interest and perseverance in my teaching ministry.

In contemporary times that special office has been smeared with charges of "Anyone can do that," "They can't do so they teach," or "That's an easy job, they don't work but nine months a year." Teachers are responsible for creatively sharing information with persons who do not want to hear them and most certainly do not want to learn. I believe that teaching is a God-ordained office. Each of us teaches, whether we want to or not. A great teacher is one who loves learning and loves people. A great teacher accepts the challenge of reaching the unreachable and teaching the unteachable. A great teacher follows the model of the Rabbi, tempering hard facts with deep love. Education is a viable space for ministry. Women may impact the church through traditional means of teaching Bible study, Sunday school, and children's church. They also can apply their skills through presenting workshops and seminars, through distance learning, seminary, Bible college, and self-study as well as via credentialing and degree acquisition.

Another locus of ministry is writing. My first published work was a collaboration of sorts. I was in the midst of writing the final draft of my dissertation, relocating to Atlanta, beginning my teaching position, and completing the requirements for my doctor of philosophy degree when I received an invitation from Dr. Ella Pearson Mitchell to submit a sermon manuscript for the second volume of her series, *Those Preaching Women*. I submitted the first draft and it came back bleeding and editorialized to a point that I was devastated. I refused to make corrections and resubmit the work with the editor's suggestions. My research assistant, Kimberely Deathrage, very calmly insisted that I needed to be published and that the collection was a prime opportunity. After a few days of my pouting and getting my ego in check, Kim assisted me in making the corrections. I learned about how to write for editors, take ownership of my creative abilities, listen nonjudgmentally to the opinions of those who initially read my work, and not fear the critique of subsequent readers. That submission, "Remember Who Made Us," opened the doors to the published writing aspect of my call.

The voices of women, particularly in religious writing, have been silent for too long. Writing is not an easy enterprise. It takes time, discipline, passion, and willingness to be vulnerable. Still, the world needs to hear the thoughts, beliefs, opinions, and ideas of women of faith. Women can work toward living out their calls through writing and publishing spiritual narratives, novels, workshop materials, church school curricula, sermon collections, grants, church administration guidelines, liturgical plays, litanies, theology books, prayer books, and a host of other areas. It is a way to tell the world what you know and believe. It is not about quick-sell, inch-deep theology, and rehashed vapid tomes. It is a means of raising your voice in a more permanent way.

The place of ministry may not be an alternative space. There are numerous denominational bodies that affirm women's calls. A woman supported at her home church can be a productive staff member. This includes operating under the supervision of a senior pastor or board. This means being compliant with the rules and regulations set forth in one's ordination covenant or the assigned pastor's program. One operates as an associate, not as the senior pastor or leader of a small clique within a larger church. If a woman is treated as an equal in her denomination, then the course of her ministry is determined by the specificity of her call.

An ongoing location of ministry for women is that of guest speaker for Women's Days, revivals, and conferences. One should be selective in accepting engagements. Avoidance of burnout and ministerial fatigue begins with proper spacing of events based on, among other things, your energy and ability to adequately prepare. Consider if the location supports women only on special days or as an integral aspect of the life of the church. What does your presence say about women in ministry or women called by God? Are you prepared to be both received and resented? Does the purpose of the engagement allow you to maintain your value system and integrity? How much information do you have about the people with whom you will be preaching? Is the ministry you will perform more important than the honorarium? Are there places you will not go? How do you wish to be introduced? How well do you handle time zone changes? Would you like to rest the night before an engagement? Are you up to participating in other activities prior to your assigned duty? Do you have allergies about which your host should be apprised before you preach or lecture? Are you prepared to wear a lapel microphone, manipulate a handheld microphone, or do you prefer a fixed microphone? There are no right or wrong answers to these questions. The bottom line is that you do not walk into a guest situation void of information about the context of your ministry.

Younger women in ministry or women beginning the process of being a guest preacher or teacher often request assistance with the business of negotiating with host churches and conferences.

The honorarium is determined by the presenter/preacher's visibility, ecclesial status and education level, length of ministry and overall qualifications for the task, years in ministry, professional affiliations, publications, church/event budget, amount of time and number of presentations/sermons, familiarity with the host, size of the congregation, travel distance and time, and others on the program on participating in the conference. I find it helpful to have a business manager or secretary negotiate the honorarium. This allows the preacher/presenter to focus on the work at hand and not dollars and cents.

I have modified my engagement request form several times over the years as I have developed more experience about the details of being a guest preacher or conference presenter. Following an invitation, I enclose this form with my biographical sketch and picture either in "snail mail" or as an e-mail attachment. I generally fill in my phone numbers and frequent flyer numbers. I am certain you can modify it to fit your particular needs.

Rev. Pastor, Bishop (appropriate title) _____ ,
Thank you for the invitation to be a part of your special event. I pray God's blessings on all the preparation and the communion of saints who will assemble on the designated day. This is a brief listing of personal requests regarding my participation.

- I require only room temperature, preferably bottled, water for preaching or speaking.
- Please let me know if I am to wear a robe, special color, or other particular attire.
- Are there specific participation expectations? Am I to only preach or speak?
- What is the proposed length of the presentation, sermon, lecture, seminar, workshop, or speech?
- Are projectors, overheads, or other presentation audio-visual equipment provided?

- If a W-9 or other tax information is required, please forward it to my home address at your earliest convenience. I prefer to receive remuneration prior to or immediately following the end of my responsibility. If you follow another process, please let me know before the event.

- Should the event require travel, please forward directions to your location.

- Should air travel be necessary, I prefer that the persons inviting me make the reservations. I prefer a window seat for comfort. I have frequent flyer accounts with Delta Airlines and United Airlines. Please contact me for the number.

- If possible, please let me know who will be picking me up at the airport and where I am to meet them. This is particularly important when I travel at night.

- Should there be a delay, I travel with my cell phone and always take some work with me so I can be productive during the wait.

- Will there be transportation back to the airport in ample time to clear security and make my plane?

- If I am to drive my private vehicle or take a shuttle, please forward mileage reimbursement information.

- If I am required to drive from the airport to the site of the event, please include rental car information and directions in your correspondence.

- I have a nonsmoking room preference. I also request that the room not be near an exit or stairway due to security concerns.

- Please let me know what payment arrangements have been made for the room. I have had several experiences where the hotel requested that I pay for the room only to discover that the group has already done so.

- Do my accommodations include meals?

- Do my accommodations include computer, Internet, or printing access?

- Should dinner or a luncheon be scheduled, I am on a restricted diet and am unable to eat spicy or fried foods and pork.
- I am unable to eat prior to preaching. Are there accommodations for a meal following the event?
- Should you request my providing books or other media for sale, I would like a projected number of copies to be ordered and shipped as well as a written guarantee of reimbursement of an agreed-upon number of products.
- If the event is postponed or cancelled, please contact me at your earliest convenience.

Thank you again for the invitation. I trust that you take these requests in the spirit in which they are intended.

The list may change depending on your experience level. I include even seemingly mundane questions. Find out the nearest drug store, hospital, or shopping center in case you leave some toiletry at home, become ill, or need extra hosiery. If you have had a long flight, ask for time to rest even if the hosts have planned a big dinner. Your ministry is more important than social time. Be gracious and send apologies to anyone who had planned on entertaining you, but get your rest. Due to limited budget, some people ask if you can stay in a private home. If there is no alternative ask for a floor or room away from everyone else and a private bath. This is important because you might not enjoy sleeping in the same room with a grandmother or children. You also need a space to meditate or to finish your sermon or production. In like manner, make certain your food choices are known. Nothing puts a damper on a presentation like food poisoning or an allergic reaction to something you ate. Try not to act like a demanding diva. You are a guest in someone's "home." Failure to use proper etiquette may result in lack of inclusion on future guest lists. The essential point is to protect yourself and insure that you have adequate space to prepare to give your gift back to God.

MOTHER WIT AND SISTAH SENSE

Reverend sister girlfriend, listen to what they never tell you in seminary or the church—Mother Wit. Sistah Sense truisms, musings, and lessons on alternate pulpits:

1. You are the first and foremost public relations agency for your ministry.
2. Establish sound relationships with the persons who invite you to minister. It is their assigned responsibility. Treat it with respect.
3. There are other chairs besides the big chair.
4. Ministry did not begin and end with you. Do not believe your own press.
5. All ground, every speck of dust God created, is holy. Ministry locations have no limits.
6. Preach to yourself, especially if you have no scheduled engagements.
7. Do not be afraid to ask to be treated like a human being.
8. Negotiate honoraria with integrity.
9. Believers in smaller churches need to hear from God just as much as believers in larger churches.
10. If God did not guarantee you a "megaministry" when you were called, work with those faithful few until God does.
11. Being a diva means high maintenance and short life span. The world does not revolve around us, regardless of the hype of the special nature of ministry.
12. Practice being a supportive staff person so when you have your own place of ministry you will be able to recognize good staff persons.
13. Ask God to muffle the voices of the naysayers so you can hear God's directives more clearly.
14. Travel light. Waiting for a ride while maneuvering three suitcases for a weekend trip can be hazardous to your health.

15. Ministry foci change due to changing demographics, staff, and opportunity.

I preached the following sermon excerpt at the Annual Seven Women at the Cross Service at Spelman College in April 2005. It speaks to women carving out their own space under God's direction. The focus text is Mark 16:1.

WHEN GOD FLIPS THE SCRIPT

Our lives at times seems like partisan political decided, Hollywood directed, media defined, and advertisement driven scripts of what it means to be fully human or socially acceptable.

Media moguls devise mindlessly scripted so-called "reality" programming of persons seemingly in peril, eating gut-wrenching insects and rodents, swinging over canyons, living with strangers—valueless, "endangered" life and limb scenarios; prescripted contest winners of viewer-logged Idols, Models, Mates; commercialized needs for extreme, nip-and-tuck, airbrushed improvements on God-created temples so that we all look alike.

Governments spend countless dollars to enact laws on who is human, what we think, how we dress, what we say, how we use our bodies, when we live, and when we die.

At times it is as if we are actors, mere puppets, or performers on a huge stage waiting to speak our lines according to someone else's script, dancing to someone else's tune, reading someone else's blueprint, living someone else's life.

Letting others:

- define our family structure,
- determine our intellectual capacity,
- delineate our economic strength,
- regulate our advancement,
- restrict our communication,

- restrain our belief ,
- reject who we are.

We are afraid to do what we know we are to do as God's
daughters and sons.

We parade around letting our past abort our future.

We walk around as if we were Jesus.

We live as spiritual somnambulists, sleepwalking through life.

We exist as spiritual couch potatoes, refusing to get up to turn
the channel from death to life.

We try to walk over other believers.

We stroll in someone else's shoes.

We are so busy following those who have written themselves
into the lead role as self-made leader, king, priest,
prophet, savior that we forget our God-scripted divine
mission to go and tell the world that he is alive.

Our focus text provides an alternative to human-directed,
prescribed, commercialized, commanded life for God's
daughters and sons.

In the first century women were second-class citizens with
few rights.

They were viewed as appendages of men rather than having
intelligence or the potential to be part of God's reign—
denigrated, dismissed, disrespected disenfranchised
eye candy,
counted after livestock and children in census of the
children of God.

Their principle function was to provide children to keep the
family lineage continuous.

But God flipped the script.

Jesus stepped over societal and cultural restrictions to minister
as he saw fit.

He talked openly with women although it was forbidden for
rabbis to speak to women in public.

He encouraged women to follow him.

He responded to their needs and saw them as persons created in God's image.

He delivered them from all types of individual and communal "dis-eases." Some were released from spiritual demons—spiritual divination, rejection of faith, half-hearted worship, false praise.

Some were freed from emotional demons—constant crying, loss of self-respect, fear of others, pity parties.

Some were healed from physical demons—muteness, blindness, seizures, insomnia, self-inflicted wounds.

Some were released from social demons—dwelling in unclean places, abuse, oppression, domestic violence, objectification.

These women began:

- sleeping outside their comfort zones,
- learning that God is the creator and sustainer of metamorphosis—of new ways of doing things, new thoughts, new relationships, new lives,
- allowing God's change agent to work within them each day,
- placing their lives before God as an offering,
- engaging internal and external evil,
- looking Satan in the face and saying, "You can't have me, I belong to God,"
- learning to live by God's standards, not the world's customs,
- feeding enemies,
- praying for those who despitefully abused them,
- laughing when their friends were happy,
- weeping when they were sad.

Women who lived in gratitude no matter what the cost.

Unusual sisters who heard the voice of Jesus say, "Come unto me and rest" and would not turn back.

Bodacious sisters who had been transformed from who they were into those pressing toward the mark of who God desired them to be.

Jesus was never bound by the social conventions that were de-
signed to keep women in places and spaces.
There is no record of women rejecting Jesus' ministry.
Jesus' message of salvation was enough to transform their lives.
Jesus taught them that God—not society, not culture, not
church—was in control of their very lives.

But God flipped the script.

Women, God's daughters:

- once weak,
- once faithless,
- once oppressed,
- once ostracized,
- once hated,
- once ridiculed,
- once shivering in the darkness,
- bumping into projections of pain,
- stumbling over broken spiritual furnishing,
- running into walls of separation,
- looking for God in all the wrong places,
- waiting outside the tombs of disappointment,
- looking inside but seeing nothing,
- sitting in silence,
- cowering in immobility,
- living in fear . . .

. . . were given the same rights as those who once controlled
them.
Jesus' presence stripped away the veneer of their socially stig-
matized personhood and taught them to live as God's
daughters of dust and deliverance.
They began to understand that they did not have to live under
their birthright as God's daughters.

That they too were made in God's image.

Women who understood that Jesus was no respecter of persons.

That this Jesus represented God's justice tempered with God's mercy.

That Jesus valued them as whole persons.

Jesus came to turn the world and its pitiful dehumanizing rule upside down.

Jesus, the Christ, their friend, the one they had followed all the way from Galilee, endured.

Women with Jesus had private conversations with one who listened and granted them favor for their obedience.

They breathed in the Spirit of a God, who opened windows of heaven and poured out blessings over and over and over again.

They also knew that they had a duty, an obligation to follow Jesus until the end of their lives.

So at the break of day, just as the sun was pushing the last bit of darkness from the sky, three days after the crucifixion, the beginning of the week after the Sabbath (rest from labor, a day refreshment of the body and blessing of the soul), three women continued their journey with Jesus:

- Mary Magdalene, the leading female disciple,
- Salome, mother of James and John, Jesus' aunt, married to Zebedee,
- Mary, mother of James the Younger and Joseph, married to husband Cleopus.

They had heard the hammering, smelled the dust, witnessed the agony, ignored the laughter, wept the tears, joined the cries, felt the earthquake—and they saw the blood, blood, drops of his blood.

They had smelled the dehydrating, sweaty skin.

These women had watched the contortions of the body as Jesus crept, bent over, along the way of suffering.

They knew what it meant to be persecuted.

They had seen where he was buried after Joseph and
Nicodemus begged his body and wrapped him in white
linens.

No autopsy, no funeral director, no lavish temple service, no
escorts to the burial site, no preacher, no ministerial staff,
no family, no resolutions, no pastoral condolences, no
flowers, no repast.

The brothers that had traveled with him were gone, the nine
that fled, the one who betrayed and committed suicide,
the one who denied knowing him, and the one who stayed
until the end and took Mary his mother home—*now gone.*

Only these women remained.

They exhibited "metamorphic boldness" (*metenoia*, repentance)
over a period of time, change from one state to another.

They became stronger because they yielded to God's will and
God's way.

Each had been grieving in her own way—in shock, confused,
guilty, hostile, in denial, immobile, angry, accepting of
what seemed at times routine.

Women who wailed, beat their breasts, tore their clothing,
put dirt on their faces, women unconcerned about what
they looked like.

They had seen the huge family sepulcher, large enough for
ten to thirteen bodies.

They knew that it would be difficult to move the stone that
sealed the tomb away, so they wondered who was going
to move it.

But they knew that they had to go to that place one more
time.

They knew the custom: one had to be buried before sundown.

That's why they started out early, before darkness gave way
to full light.

Eyes still swollen from crying jags, sleep still claiming the
corners of the eye and edges of their mouths.

Brushing the sand off their clothes from a night spent in restless, grief-stricken sleep.
They started out early to avoid the Romans who were supposed to guard his tomb.
They began before they were expected because their love said
they had to minister to the one who had saved them from
a predictable, hellish existence.

Women were often the only mourners at funerals.
Women were hired as mourners, trained in laments and
dirges, shouting "Alas, our brother" for the government's
poster boy for unpatriotic behavior.
They brought sweet burial spices of myrrh, cinnamon, cane,
cassia, and olive oil to anoint his body.
They were on their way to prepare Jesus' body for burial—

- the face that had held eyes that looked at them as human,
  not property,
- the head that had held up that crown of thorns as blood,
  sweat, and tears dripped down his cheeks,
- the hands that had touched them with care and healed
  their broken places,
- the feet—blistered, bruised, calloused—that had walked
  with them as they had journeyed from who they had been
  toward who God wanted them to become.

As they went they probably wondered who would be there to
help them move the seal from the tomb.
If they touched the stone they would defile the grave according to Jewish tradition.
God stepped in again and changed predictability.
God was present before they faced the problem of moving the
stone to open the tomb.
The text says that when they arrived at the tomb, the stone
was already rolled away.

They boldly entered the tomb, looking for their friend, their
Lord, their Savior, perhaps fearing someone had stolen
the body.
An angel of the Lord, clothed in white with a radiant face said

"Do not be afraid.
He is not here.
He has risen."

Jesus' resurrection is a *kairos* moment—when the liberating
power of God breaks into the dead places in our lives and
moves us to dedication, growth, and development.
Don't be afraid. Remember his parable about the temple
being raised in three days?
The text says Mary Magdalene, Salome, and Mary were filled
with awe and fear.
Over the years I have heard many preach that the women
were weak and afraid, that they had to tell the men, who
then would know what to say.
But what would you do if you watched a loved one die,
made all the arrangements,
went to the visitation, and saw with your own eyes that the
casket was empty
and were told, "Go home; he will be waiting for you," and
"Don't tell anyone else but the small group of believers"?
God shifted the paradigm again.
Jesus came to save all sinners.
Mary Magdalene, Salome, and Mary were ordained right there
in the tomb, commissioned in a place that was once filled
with death to spread the news about new life:

- no laying on of hands by elders,
- no robes, rings, or stoles,
- no board of examiners to question their call and anointing,
- no deacons meeting to test their efficiency,
- no church vote,

- just a divine ordination to go tell the disciples and Peter he has gone to Galilee, he'll meet them there.

God flipped the script.

Sisters were amazed; they trembled, filled with fear.
The angel did not say, "Go tell the other sisters";
not "Sell your story to *Today, GMA,* CNN, or Fox";
not "Go tell your husband, significant other, or pastor";
not "Wait until you are given a book deal or movie rights are secured or a resurrection DVD is released."
These women who had been healed of demons were sent to tell the good news to men who had denied Christ and abandoned their faith—all sinners saved by grace.
BUT "Go tell my disciples, the ones who ran away, the ones who were too afraid of societal reprisals to own me, the ones I lived outside with for three years, ate with, and whose feet I washed.
Go tell the other disciples and Peter, the one who denied me three times.
Go tell everyone else I am risen.
Go and tell them that I did just what I said I would do.
Go and tell them that the papers were wrong, Jesus is not dead; he is alive.
Go tell them."

God knows the law says women are to keep quiet in public, but go anyway.
God knows that some will try to kill you for speaking, but tell it anyway.
God knows that some will not believe you, but witness anyway.
God knows some will believe you are trying to assume someone else's part, but proclaim anyway.
God knows that some will say you are stepping out of your place, but sing it anyway.

God knows that some will turn away because they will think
    you are possessed, but deliver the Word of life anyway.
He is not here; he has risen.
Jesus was resurrected, reanimated, regenerated, resuscitated
    for imperfect people just like us.
Some have social problems.
But Jesus repaired the breach of covenant relationship.
But Jesus refinanced the mortgage of bankrupt spirituality.
Some have physical diseases.
But Jesus reoriented the minds of objectified humanity.
But Jesus rekeyed the doors of obstructed opportunity.
Some have emotional issues.
But Jesus released the captives of self-initiated addictions.
But Jesus replenished the landscape of polluted creation—
like the sisters at the tomb,
like you and like me, earthen vessels, sinners saved by
    God's grace,
sisters and brothers who have come short of God's glory,
ordinary people whom God uses to do great things, whom
    God allows to live as God's daughters and sons
I'm glad that God—
not government, not media, not society, not church, not
    school, not home—God sets the standard for our
    humanity.
I'm glad that Jesus—
not some cyberspace, celluloid, choreographed, cloned,
    castigating, calculating human creator—is the author and
    finisher of our faith and our fate.
God—through the power of the Holy Spirit in Jesus—
flipped our scripts.
When we should have been dead in our sins,
God wrote a new chapter.
When we did not know how to pray for ourselves,
God edited the book of life.
Now we have to go tell others that he is alive. Amen.

There is a saying that "your gifts will make room for you." In my mind this means we should not worry about human constructed barriers but look for alternate routes to our particular work site. It may take more time, but we will get there. God will ask why we did not complete our assignments. Did we do what is outlined in Luke 4:18–19 and proclaim good news in the midst of so much verbal manipulation and purposeful functional atheism? Did we work to end alienation, mendacity, prejudice, oppression, and ostracism? Did we try to envision what could be, not just what was? Did we assist others in clarity of their own vision? Did we work just as hard for one as we did for one thousand? Did we do the ministry to which we were called? When we have finished our assignment through death or a decision to pursue other vocations, the reward is not what people say, but what God says. God already has gifted us with the tools to do the work. It is up to us to use them. What will your work say for you?

Peace,
Teresa

SEVEN

SWIMMING WITH SHARKS BUT SAFELY REACHING THE SHORE

Dear Water of Life Aficionados,

Sisters, I love water. Summers in my childhood were spent at my grandparents' houses in Sedalia, Missouri. Monday through Saturday we went swimming, after lying down an hour after lunch, at C.C. Hubbard Park. Just one block from both sets of grandparents, the park was the hub of the Black ("Colored" at that time) community. Preachers, teaches, mechanics, cooks, laborers, and their families knew that the only hierarchy in the water was determined by swimming expertise. To me there has always been something not only cleansing but also adventurous about my body moving through water, something comforting about floating in the water, something challenging about pushing myself to go deeper each time I entered a pool—without of course ignoring the safety regulations posted all around me. I sense the same attraction to ministry.

I feel differently in bodies of water that are not contained and maintained like a swimming pool. I do not enjoy swimming in the ocean. I am never sure of just how deep the bottom is or what is navigating the deep. I find myself swimming close to the shore where I am able to see and feel what is just beneath me. No matter how much my family cajoles me, I stick to what I know for sure. I know that part of my reticence stems from watching the Discovery Channel's shark week programming and from late night viewing of *Jaws* I, II and III.

Last year I purchased a season pass for the Atlanta Aquarium. I am fascinated by what I cannot ordinarily see with the naked eye. The fish are contained and no matter how big they are they cannot hurt me. It was while studying the shark that metaphors of ministry flooded my mind. Sharks are predators.[1] We will encounter people who look out for themselves. They will try to destroy or hurt anything and anyone who stands between them and their goal. Some will use written and unwritten rules to ban us. There are people who smell our blood, our sweat, our tears, or who sense our pain while we are swimming upstream without a boat or a paddle. They may be alone or have a group of pilot fish or remora who watch but do not contribute anything but a smile or curiosity. Other sharks accidentally attack us due to our association with someone else, belief in some errant information, or as part of their collateral damage. The most common such shark attack is due to territorialism, like a sister who believes you are trying to usurp her power or enter her space. I know most people think that church is a safe space. I would agree for the most part, but my experience teaches that sharks are in both shallow and deep ecclesial waters. Some sharks coexist peacefully with us, accepting or ignoring our presence.

---

1. See http://www.flmnh.ufl.edu/fish/Sharks/sharks.htm or http://new-brunswick.net/new-brunswick/sharks/types.html for a more extensive discussion of sharks.

Others are ready and willing to attack even as we do what God has appointed. Like the little fish in the Pixar cartoon, *Finding Nemo*, we have to stay in the water and swim for our lives or get out of the pool, dry off, and go home.

The location of most of our ministry is the institutional church. It is more than a building. It is more than an institution. It is composed of imperfect people. The church is social. The church is a living organism teeming with human emotions and actions. The church is spiritual. Generally the life of the church focuses on the interrelationship of God, others, and self. The church is political. Guidelines, rules, laws, polity, disciplinary restrictions, and spur of the moment judgments or actions by persons who seek to stop or block our progress are inherent to the system.

Successfully navigating sociopolitical waters in ministry begins with accepting that ministry is no easy journey. The journey is not only through placid times in which it appears that everything and everyone is affirming us; it is also fraught with perfect storms where it appears that everything and everyone is working against us. In the midst of it all we must be diligent in the pursuit of our ministries regardless of the particular location and the variety of sharks that surround us. Some persons will seek to exploit our gifts, perhaps by assigning us to work a sixty-hour week with no pay. Some will marginalize us based on our gender or their fear of our abilities, all the time remarking that Black women have more privileges than Black men. Some will resort to a form of cultural imperialism, ascribing characteristics that define us as the intrusive "other" that seeks to deny them their "rights," the one who is never good enough to be equal to them. Some will use systemic violence such as physical intimidation, public character assassination, or comparisons to other women who have been unsuccessful in ministry to calcify our resolve and leave us with a sense of powerlessness. These actions are like the thresher shark that slaps the surface of the water with its fin, causing the smaller fish to rush together so it can whip or stun them into confusion and then kill them as they cower in fear. When the world around us is shaking, the best thing we can do is evaluate the cause and calmly evacuate even as others want to stay. Remember you may not be the focus of the attack. You may simply be in the area and receive the brunt of the action. One can usually return later, survey the damage, and rebuild in the same or a different location.

The good news is that there are infinite possibilities for living above these maneuverings and finishing our course. The good news is that God never calls us to failure. The good news is that the church ultimately belongs to God, not to people. The good news is that God called us, not boards, committees, or family members. The good news is that with proper safety measures we will reach the shore in spite of the sharks.

The great white shark in the ministerial pool is sexism. Sexism is often a solitary predator. It is cosmopolitan in nature, purposefully seeking in this instance women in ministry. Like the great white seeking its prey, sexism has five stages: detection of a target, identification of the person's strengths and weaknesses, approach toward the usually solitary individual, subjugation of the person or persons with seduction, power plays, or threats, and insidious consumption of the heart, mind, and soul.

In the form of sexual harassment such attacks may come as verbal intimidation, such as jokes about bodies, intrusive inquiries regarding your sex life, assumptive proclamations about your sexuality, or sanctions about women congregating. Sexual misconduct is sometimes subtle and sometimes blatant. The goal is disempowerment, removing confidence, breaking resolve, inculcating fear, dismantling courage, and stifling voice. The conspiracy of silence and culture of shame make it difficult for women to name this evil and to deal with its consequences. Promises of promotions or threats of barriers silence the most vocal temporarily or at times permanently. The great white is then able to continue trawling for more prey.

In my home conference there was a pastor who told women entering ministry that if they associated with any women in ministry organizations he would personally see to it that they would never be ordained. His premise was that women's organizations were antimale lesbian sex clubs. The additional horror of his actions was that the denominational leadership knew what he was doing and looked the other way. He publicly praised women or credited himself with their advancement as long as bishops were present but privately whispered in their ears or in staff meetings, demeaning their gifts.

In other instances there are derogatory comments made regarding a woman's physical characteristics associated with her entrance or advancement into ministry. Is she easy on the eyes? Is she pretty enough to be on a ministerial staff or in a denominational office? Does she look like a man? Is she too old to change? Comments about her sexual prowess may be fodder for the old boys' network. I remember entering an office filled with male clergy who were engaged in uproarious laughter and back slapping. The hooting began to subside but the known womanizer without looking up continued his description of a woman's derriere and what he would give to be with her for five minutes. Throats began to clear as he launched deeper into his fantasy of how much she would enjoy him since women in ministry do not have sex. Finally one of the men spoke up with "Bru, Bru, that's enough." As the minister looked up he stopped in mid-sentence and shifted to "Oh, Teresa knows I was just kidding. I didn't mean no harm." My initial thoughts were "What a fool." I could not help but wonder how many women he actually approached with his self-proclaimed talents and his project to "lay hands on as many desperate women in ministry as God would allow." As an older male minister once told me, "Fry, remember if you ever say yes to a promotion while on your back, your name will be written in every men's room in the A.M.E. Church. Let God use your gifts to promote you." In my mind this translated into the abuser winning and my name potentially becoming synonymous with either weakness or prostitution. I had no intention of selling my self to anyone. I knew that God had made me stronger than that.

Some leave ministry never receiving any healing of their pain or shame. At times even other women do not believe what you are going through or that the person or persons you name could be involved in such a thing. There is a curious belief even in the twenty-first century that women are the initiators of any sexual activity. Submission to male leadership continues to mean that women are inferior and deserve whatever happens to them. Some pursue denominational channels to address publicly the predator. I am aware that some women comply with sexual propositions and so advance in ministry. I have no way of knowing what works for whom. The course of action and the repercussions are personal matters. Some women reject sexual advances and find alternate routes in ministry. This may manifest itself in leaving the church altogether or developing coping mechanisms of denial, avoidance, or self-deprecation. Other women address the sexual advance, stay in the church, deal with the consequences of their actions, and keep moving. Regardless of one's choice, in order for you to stay on course it is essential to know the denominational policies on sexual harassment or misconduct, seek a cohort of women and men who understand what you are encountering, and work through the spiritual, psychological, emotional, and sometimes physical wounds. If we are fortunate, others will help carry us back to the shore and stay with us until we are able to swim again.

Sometimes we have to avoid scavengers that seek to take what God has blessed us with in ministry. They are similar to the slow swimming basking shark that feeds on the residue of the gifts and talents of others. They are rarely dangerous and generally tolerant of others. They swim near the surface with their mouths open, catching everything they can. They may seek to make others pay for what they are not. In the ordination process, there may be members on the examining boards who experienced deficits in their training or were treated objectionably in their journey through ordination. Their assignment seems to be to make our lives a living hell. No matter what we

do, they have a comment. No matter how hard we try, they say
we are not doing enough. They somehow think nothing of bor-
rowing our comments, copying sermon notes, and even mim-
icking our mannerisms to enhance their ministries. There is an
expectation that we become a "clean-up woman." We are to
make everything work well but receive no credit and have no
comment on the theft of our creative material. Why? We are
too grateful merely for the opportunity to serve.

I have preached revivals where someone comes up and asks
for my manuscript so they can use it the following Sunday. While
I am grateful that the words were understood and I must admit
that I feel complimented by the praise, I am a little miffed that
the request would result in someone preaching verbatim what I
had slaved over. I do not mind loaning pieces—most preachers
do so—but please give credit where credit is due. Having a company of preachers you trust is a great protection from scavengers. I was advised to at least refer the person requesting my
manuscript to purchase the tape and transcribe it. There is little
protection for creative work, but at least make them work for it.
My preaching friends also act as a sounding board when I need
to work through my disdain for lazy preachers. Confession is
good for the soul. There have been times when I deliberately
omitted parts of sermons in the versions that are published just
so people have to do a bit of research to preach it effectively.
Womanist ethicist Katie Cannon advised me early in my ministry to learn the rules of the adversary well enough to use them
to your advantage. Sometimes you have to feed the scavengers
the wrong menu or at least one with fewer nutrients.

Sometimes the scavengers are like the remoras that accompany some sharks.[2] They may attach themselves to the shark
and survive by feasting off the leftovers from the shark's mouth.
A tragic irony of ministry is that some of our worst enemies are
other sisters. Some sisters believe that the only way they can get

---

2. http://www.britannica.com/eb/article-9063158/remora.

ahead is to play the game like brothers. They will do anything and everything to win the approval of the men even if it means trying to kill off whomever they perceive to be their female opponent. Discerning the motive of these sisters is difficult; after all, aren't we supposed to be supportive of each other? We may assume they have our best interests at heart until they begin to share confidential information with others, like inside sources leaking secrets in Washington. When you encounter a sister who gives you worn tools, then stays around for your funeral, pray for her first. Some sisters are minions who survive on miniscule rewards for their actions. Quite honestly, some sisters show up only for photo ops after you have done all the work. If God has blessed you to stand at the front of the line today, let the sister stand with you. In some cases it may be the only opportunity she will ever have. Remember, when you were ascending, someone let you stand in their picture.

Finally remora should remember they are not the shark. Avoidance of assimilation or cooptation of shark behavior means survival of your true self. Missing a meal every now and then does not hurt anyone.

The sociopolitical systems of churches rarely are construed as female-dominated and -controlled entities. There are ordination riptides, local church turbulence, staff waves, and role definition whirlpools to watch, avoid, or ride out. Occasionally, even in calm water, there may be an occasional tiger shark that jumps out of the water, catching us off guard. Tiger sharks are typically sluggish swimmers but move quickly at feeding time. Once you have spotted them, keep potential tiger sharks in view at all times. There is an old saying that you have to keep your friends close and your enemies closer. Just when you think you know your call is to the ordination process, tiger sharks of personal illness, family difficulty, financial imbalance, or denominational changes may appear on the horizon. We may be so unprepared that we suffer injury. Critical care is necessary. No time to wait for outside help. Save yourselves before things deteriorate.

I have learned that one can avoid time in the critical care unit if one remembers to read the small print of the discipline, polity, or church law. Take some time and familiarize yourself with your denominational history. Know what women preceded you. Ask those you trust how they negotiated the life of the church. Investigate for yourself which brothers support you and which ones seek women's heads on a platter. Set your own boundaries and do not let anyone move the markers. You know your own safety zone. To avoid role confusion always remember that although you may do the bulk of the work unless you are the assigned pastor, you have power but no authority. If the sharks are in the middle of the ocean, move to the shoreline. Remember, you need to be aware of your surroundings even in the church. At times we forget that the same people we encounter in the world, we also see inside the walls of the church. The difference is the language we use. I have watched too many women let their guard down because someone shouted "Jesus." When this happens some sisters do not realize they have been bitten until their hearts stop.

Sometimes there is a person swimming next to you who shouts a warning of imminent danger or tries to take the pain of the shark's attack away. I reminisce about the lessons taught by Rev. Daryl Walker. He is one of those rare souls who remembered how such a brutal process can end in beauty. He would stop by during those four to five hours a small group of black clad ordinands waited in sweltering August heat to be interrogated by ordained clergy. He would tell stories, do impressions, make jokes, and ask about our families. In that intimate space we felt like we could make it. We trusted him enough to be ourselves, and he extended himself enough to help us navigate the currents. Some were consumed by the sharks. Some stopped swimming and disappeared. Some of us made it out alive and are in ordained ministry today. At the end of the day, each of us had to learn to swim alone. We each had to resolve conflict and confusion using our personal wit and perseverance. We each needed to trust that the shoreline was within our reach.

Although many sharks are predatory, the whale shark is relatively harmless. The largest fish in the world, whale sharks are curious. The whale shark exemplifies the essence of ministry. I have come to understand that most congregants are harmless. They attend services to assist them in navigating their own route toward the shore. It is difficult to believe at times but for some congregants having women in ministry is still unusual and misunderstood. They have little personal experience with women as pastors or preachers. They have heard about women in ministry, but until like Doubting Thomas they see, hear, touch and feel for themselves, they are unable to make an informed decision about your qualifications. Some sisters arrive ready to do battle and there is no war. I have preached at predominately White churches where no one but the person who invited me shook my hand or spoke to me until after the service. The word of God is a marvelous equalizer and barrier breaker. I have preached at predominately Black churches where I was "the first and only" woman to have been allowed in the pulpit. Following the service I was told, "I am not much for women preachers but you are an exception to the rule." I always wondered who wrote the rule and if another woman would be preaching there. All I know is that whatever I do the sister who follows me will be compared to that standard. I try to avoid having her clean up a mess I made.

How do women in ministry begin to transform shark behavior and resolve conflict surrounding our ministries? The answer depends on your place of ministry. My doctoral work was in individual and social transformation. I know that in order for society to change individuals must first change. Effective change is never dictated but is always a process of discarding the old, often pain-filled behaviors and deciding to develop new life-giving behaviors. The responsibility for change that opens the way for women in ministry to do what

God is telling them cannot be done with women alone. In partnership with like-minded men, women can begin to confront "powers and principalities" that restrict women's personhood. We each have a duty to name the offense, the evil, the shark, and then plot ways to either avoid them or obliterate them. If this seems impossible we either adapt to the environment or move. Transformation happens at different times for different people. There are no magic formulas or short answers. Change is painful for both the person being restricted and the one who creates the restrictions.

I like the what the late Audre Lourde said: "It is learning how to stand alone, unpopular and sometimes reviled, and how to make common cause with those others identified as outside the structures in order to define and seek a world in which we can all flourish. It is learning how to take our differences and make them strengths. For the master's tools will never dismantle the master's house."[3] Individually or collectively women in ministry should build alliances with others who are on the same course we walk. We have to build trust as we go. Disappointments will come, but just keep working. We release the temptation to do unto others what they have done. The process is time consuming, but at least all our energies will not be exhausted fighting an often invisible enemy. Proactive action rather than reaction is ultimately more satisfying and less frustrating. Remember that every sister needs courage to stand for herself. One cannot afford to use the same tools or methods that were used before. One must creatively tailor tools of transformation to fit one's current situation.

Bishop John R. Bryant invited me to preach at an ordination service held on September 9, 2006 at the Midwest Annual Conference of the Fifth Episcopal District of the African Methodist Episcopal Church in Kansas City, Kansas. The focus

---

3. Audre Lourde, *Sister Outsider* (Trumansburg, N.Y.: Crossing Press, 1984), 40–112.

texts were 2 Samuel 23:20–23 and 2 Corinthians 6:1–10. The title of the sermon was "On-the-Job Courage." This is an excerpt of that sermon dealing with the navigation of political waters and being faithful to one's ordination covenant.

ON-THE-JOB COURAGE

Ministry at one time was perceived as an honorable and noble profession.

There was honor and respect afforded the sacrificial work and social consciousness of John Jasper, Richard Allen, Jarena Lee, Reverdy Ramson, Julia Foote, Henry McNeil Turner, Vernon Johns, Harry Hooper, Adam Powell, Martin King, Prathia Hall, Frederick Sampson, and the like. Men and women who understood that ministry is learned in God's crucible of life experience—

- no shortcuts,
- no do-overs,
- no excuses,
- no clones,
- no easy road,
- called to a higher standard,
- already in the not yet,
- can't hear nobody pray,
- in spite of,
- anyhow,
- sacrifice and reward,
- trial and error,
- success and defeat,
- pain-and-gain ministry.

Not a day goes by without the ministry or work of some contemporary pastor, preacher, minister, bishop, prelate, primate, archbishop, pope, evangelist, apostle, prophet, prophetess, missionary, or self-proclaimed king or queen of life becoming the subject of:

- an Internet blog,
- a message board discussion,
- a news update,
- a social commentary,
- a blistering editorial,
- a parking lot patter,
- hallway hollahs,
- restaurant rhetoric,
- a text message,
- an airport appellation.

Descriptors of twenty-first century ministers are often reduced to comedic derision and celluloid caricatures of men and women:

- hungry for chicken,
- arrayed in outlandish cabaret-like attire,
- touting affected spiritual gifts for sale,
- scamming or manipulating congregational funds,
- demanding sexual favors.

In reality, some of those who say they are called by God to preach, to minister, to lead God's people waste time and God's precious gift by critiquing other people's lives:

- what they think,
- who they love,
- where they went to school,
- what size church they lead,
- who has the most hits on their website,

- who chooses to teach rather than pastor,
- who has the favor of the bishop,
- who gets to sit in the big chair,
- whose voice sounds like a preacher,
- who has the right hair style,
- who's in whose clique.

These people spend insufficient time on their own assignment. Some in our profession are spiritually aquaphobic, afraid of the water—afraid of the spiritual, social, political, or intellectual aspects of ministry. This leaves them prone to:

- construction of Nebuchadnezzar-like cathedrals on urban and exurban Plains of Dura, with subsequent mandates that all fall down in submission to their greatness,
- dispensing dumbed-down inch-deep theological messages with salvation as an afterthought,
- hawking their latest self-help manual or their ghost-written, published-last-night gospel as the latest *rhema* word,
- heavy bass crossover vapid theology lyrics rather than the biblically based songs of Zion,
- consumer driven programs rather than social justice ministries,
- seeking the path of least resistance,
- getting lost in the crowd,
- imitating humans instead of God,
- avoidance of public profession for faith or private confession of belief,
- muting their own voices,
- coveting someone else's gifts,
- fear of failure,
- fear of success,
- never taking a stand on anything,

- straddling the fence on every issue waiting to see which way the people in presumed power vote.

One would think that with the exponential proliferation of gigachurch ministries—

- international televangelism networks,
- cyberspace ministries,
- CD, DVD, cassettes, new books, and billboards—

everyone and everything in the world would be saved and sanctified.
One would think that:

- there would not be one person who did not know about Jesus,
- the name of Jesus would be on everyone's lips,
- there would not be wars,
- all of God's sons and daughters would be in line to go to heaven,
- everyone would be pressing toward the mark of the high calling,
- all of us would value the sacrifice of God's only Son for our liberty.

One would think, be led to believe, agree . . . were that the case.
One would think we could just close up our Bibles,
stop praying,
and know that we are all set to gather up our new robe, ring, shoes, and wings and to walk golden streets,
sit at the welcome table,
and see Jesus face to face.
One might be led to believe that ministry is irrelevant.
One might think that ministry is too much hassle.
One might think that.
One would think . . .

But God says there is much work to do.
Stop, look, listen:

- Too many are ambulating in apathy.
- Too many are promenading in pride.
- Too many are rambling in rage.
- Too many are sauntering in sin.
- Too many are pacing in poison.
- Too many are stepping in selfishness.
- Too many are treading in temptation.
- Too many are walking in wickedness.

Effective ministry, serving well, takes courage.
Courage: State or quality of mind that enables one to face
danger, fear, with self-possession, confidence, resolution.
Courage is the life-giving, life-resurrecting power of the
good news,
the saving Word,
the empowered message,
the naked truth that frees us from debilitating rumors and
unsubstantiated predictions of the demise of God's world.
Courage overshadows superficiality.
Courage to understand the power in ministry is not about
people but about God in the people.
We need a few good men and women who know the power
and paucity of ministry but enter anyway—
women and men who know that courage for this tasks lies not
in where we end but that we "faithed" enough to begin
the process,
who recognize that this ordination is a human witness to what
God has already planned for our lives.
The church needs men and women dedicated and convicted
to serve with integrity, dignity, grace, love, and loyalty,
who let nothing and nobody stop them from doing God's will,
God's way.

The world needs women and men who possess on-the-job
  courage.
In 2 Samuel, chapter 23, we find David's last words.
In a divine oracle, David reflects on his life and the realization
  that he did not succeed without the help of others.
David received the praise but God surrounded him with people, understudies, background singers, support systems,
  ministering angels, wise counselors, coworkers, adminis-
  trative staff, and body guards who has just as much
  strength and ability as he.
He was supported, ministered, protected, nurtured, counseled, and saved by a group of "mighty men of God."
Once a rag-tag army in the wilderness, they loyally followed
  the orders of the apple of God's eye from the caves of
  Addulam to the palace in Jerusalem, through

- victory and defeat,
- war and peace,
- prosperity and famine.

Their blood, sweat, isolation, pain, suffering, tears, joy, and
  love helped build a nation.
They understood David's assignment from God.
They suffered with David.
They took care of David.
They guarded his very life.
They risked their lives for his cause.
They learned to face danger and fear, with self-possession,
  confidence, and resolution while doing their jobs.
Their employee handbook was their faith.
Their battle instructions came from God's mouth.
There is no record that any of them tried to

- be David,
- write like David,
- dress like David,

- plot to take his throne,
- blog his personal life,
- sell their inheritance for instant gratification,
- spend more time working in mess than on a message,
- run away when things got a little tough.

There was an inner circle of Three Mighty Warriors.

The next level of bodyguards was called the Thirty.

One of the Thirty, Benaiah (made by God), provides a
    metaphor of on-the-job courage. 1 Samuel 23:21b:
    "He also went down and killed a lion in a pit on a day
    when snow had fallen."

He also . . .

We are told nothing about his life other than his service
    to David,

nothing other than that his father, Jehoiada, was David's
    bodyguard, chief of his mercenary corps.

In one account he went to battle with a small club, took the
    spear out of a giant's hand, and killed him.

He dedicated his life to service to the king. David evidently
    was captivated by one telling, courageous event.

He also went down . . .

Like a call—individual or corporate (gradual, nurtured, or
    cataclysmic).

We have no information about why he went down.

Like with our calls,

only God and you will ever really know your story or why you
    answered.

Who in her/his right mind would boldly set forward to be
    castigated as an impostor or pimp?

Who would willingly give up jobs, family, friends, prestige, and
    security to go to school at age 30, 40, or 50?

Who would go from one assignment to another with no guaran-
    tee of staying long enough to find the church except one
    who is called and sent by somebody greater than you or me?

What bit of insanity courses through us that we would offer
  ourselves as vessels to stand on holy ground and proclaim
  God's Word to a world that stands in darkness?
We are not told where the encounter took place,
how he arrived at the site,
whether he was alone,
whether he had properly prepared for the situation.
Like when God has sent us, moved from a safe place into
  uncharted territory—
places we never thought we would be,
spaces we said we would never occupy.
Can't remember when we said yes;
Just know that God said go and we went.
No idea if we will have enough money for the move,
or whether we will arrive safely.
Do not know who or what will meet us there.
But we go,
trusting that God is already there.
He also went down and killed a lion . . .
killed a lion
Lions (mentioned 135 times in the OT) were known for their
  strength.

- Young, swift lions were herbivores, ate only plants.
- Old lions, teeth and strength failing, carnivores, resorted
  to eating humans.
- Their lairs were in forests, caves of the mountains, on the
  banks of the Jordan.
- Hunters caught them in pits or with bow and arrow or nets.

We are not told why the lion was killed.
Sometimes people, places, and things are removed from our
  path and no one but God knows why.
We are not told if Benaiah was wounded in the encounter.
Some of our wounds, problems, issues, habits, and needs are
  hidden from others.

In ministry we will, like Benaiah, face lions.

David said in Psalm 57:4, "I find myself in a pride of lions who
are wild for a taste of human flesh; their teeth are lances
and arrows, their tongues are sharp daggers."

Lions that seek to kill, steal, and destroy.

Seems like as soon as we decide to follow the will of God, answer
God's call to ministry, go where God says go, do what God
says do, people come out of the woodwork to criticize us—

lions who look at the work you are doing and become jealous,

lions who can't wait to run to the bishop, senior pastor, elder,
laity, even members of your own family to

- tear down your work,
- accuse you of worshipping other gods,
- charge that you don't pray enough,
- that your hoop is insufficient,
- that you don't have the bishop's favor,
- or that you don't really believe what they believe,

lions who whisper lies, smile in your face but plot how to bring
you down,

lions who would rather gossip about you than talk with you,

lions whose appointment is to stay on your case,

lions who are ordained to start confusion,

lions who sell tickets to watch you fail,

old, tied, feeble lions who can't do the work but want you
to stop,

lions male and female who want to see you dumb and defeated,

lions who conspire to change God's assignment of your gifts
and talents

- in the work that you undertake,
- in the midst of your faithfulness,
- in the face of persons who still refuse to honor God's
creative force.

You may be wounded in the house of your friends, and
disappointment seems to be in the very air you breathe.
But the work we are assigned to do does not stop.
He also went down and killed a lion in a pit . . .
A pit: a large natural or artificial cavity or hole in the ground,
an abyss, depression, low point.
Sometimes in ministry,
when we are doing God's work,
no matter how hard we try, nothing seems to work,
attack may come from all directions.
Sometimes the pit is our own self-doubt, indecision, confusions,
   or lack of self-affirmation.
Yes, on this job there will be times of discouragement:

- times when we will feel way down yonder by ourselves and
  can't hear nobody pray,
- times people won't listen,
- times nobody comes to the meeting,
- times people will criticize everything we do,
- times when jealous folk will seek our destruction,
- times we may forget our purpose,
- times our strength will seem low,
- times when we will want to give up,
- times when we are too tired to think about getting up again,
- times when grief grips our being,
- times when even small acts seems unappreciated,
- times of sadness,
- times of fear,
- times of tears,
- times of confusion,
- times of numbness,
- times of disappointment,
- times for searching why we werecalled in the first place,

- times we know we may never become famous,
- time folk may never say thank you,
- times people may never know our names,
- times when we think we have lost our minds,
- times family and friends may think we are crazy,
- times even the church may stop supporting us.

In the pit there are options:

- Quit—join another group.
- Lie—pretend that everything is fine.
- Fight—not each other but what is wrong.
- Adapt—do what others do whether God says so or not.
- Change—let God work through us.

On-the-job courage demands that we be willing to die—risk
self and watch God move.
*He also went down and killed a lion in a pit on a day when
snow had fallen.*
. . . on a day when snow had fallen. Snow: hexagonal lattice
crystals of ice,
common in Palestine in the winter in the hills,
sometimes ranging up to two feet,
sometimes on the ground five or more days.
Banaiah was in the snow covered pit.
Like the first few years of ministry when one discovers that
the ministerial parent, board of examiners, members of
the ordination class, seminary professor, mama, and 'nem
could only teach us so much.
The rest of ministry is like a snowy day.
It looks beautiful.
It sounds tranquil.
But moving through it may be difficult one minute
and filled with the joy of snow angels the next.
We may find ourselves perhaps slipping and sliding,

perhaps crawling, falling,
perhaps with good traction,
perhaps advancing and retreating,
perhaps miscalculating the foe, then regrouping,
perhaps circling and going in a straight line,
perhaps staying for days,
perhaps removing the obstacle in minutes.
Banaiah killed the lion with the tools of his trade:

- his experience,
- his sword,
- his soldier's spirit,
- his belief in the God who kept him when he faced the giants.

I imagine he knew that the same God who kept him as David's
    bodyguard would protect him in the pit,
whatever the unexpected movement of walking on ice,
treading the path,
perhaps bloody but alive.
He reached the lion, defeated it, left the pit, and testified
    about how he got over.
There are times in ministry
when we can't seem to find anything to hold on to.
We forget that God's Word assures us that we have protection
    from slippery slopes,

- in self denial,
- in prayer and fasting,
- in shouts of joy,
- in silently waiting for such a time as this,
- in tears and sorrows,
- in fatigue and mental breakdowns,
- in burnout and effervescence,
- on the mountain top,

- and in the valley,
- when we're sick,
- when we're well,
- when we have much,
- when we have little,
- when we're alone,
- and in a crowd,
- with one or one million,
- through sickness, pain, loss, and gain,
- life and death.

I hear God's promise to Habakkuk—
make our feet like hinds' feet so we can climb out safely.
If we have the courage to enter the pit—
moving out of our comfort zones,
identifying evil and engaging it,
slipping and falling but getting up and trying it again,
doing the work of the one who sent us—
we will learn how to survive along the way,
trusting that God is still working through us, in us, around us,
in spite of us.
*He also went down and killed a lion in a pit on a day when
snow had fallen.*
Apostle Paul teaches us that ministry can be treacherous.
Risky.
Laborious.
It is not for the weak, lazy, selfish, egotistical, cowardly, whiny,
greedy, thin-skinned, or power hungry.
Paul reminds each minister that as servants of God we have
promised to commend and submit ourselves every way to
God's agenda.
We are called to serve . . . not be served.
We are bodyguards for God's church.
Forces are present that will seek to destroy our mission.

Paul writes that we will face trials, but the good news is that
   God supplies our needs through weapons cf righteousness
   for both hands.
God puts a fist in our backbones and urges us to move forward in

- knowledge,
- patience,
- kindness,
- holiness of spirit,
- genuine love,
- truthful speech, and the power of God.

God reminds us of our conviction to ministry
every time we see the face of a child who has discovered his or
   her belief in Jesus, not just the Jesus in the Sunday school
   literature, but the one in their hearts
every time a new soul is won for the cause of Christ
every time a family trusts us to pray for that dying loved one
every time we come to an annual conference and hear
   "And Are We Yet Alive?"
every time God illuminates a text and you see it in a different
   light than the last fifty times you read it
every time God preaches through you
every time your soul looks back and wonders how you got over
   and you can't help but shout
every time
every time you are healed
every time you are filled with God's Spirit
every time you thought your heart would break and you felt
   God stitch up the hole
Keep in mind that every tear you shed on the journey,
every pain you feel on the journey
every lonely night you spend on the journey,
every headache you experience on the journey,
every joy you share on the journey,

every victory you have on the journey
is all to the glory of God.
Use each success and each failure as a lesson for the next step
on the journey.
We have been given a divine assignment,
blessed by God to do work,
sent by God to use love to change the world.
Not just when all our lights turn green, but in the face of red
ones too.
Not just when our names are called, but when no one knows us.
If we do not trust God when life gets rough,
our faith will become stagnant;
our resolve will become calcified.
The lions will win.
We must pray for the perseverance to stand in the courage.
Each of us is blessed by God to work in the here and now in
preparation for reward in the then and there.
Be glad today for those with the on-the-job, in-the-trenches,
on-the-ground, until-the-end, God-ordained courage
that enables us to face danger and fear, with self possession,
confidence, and resolution.
This is our calling; this is our purpose; this is our story; this is
our responsibility.
We are called to serve well—
to kill the lions in the middle of the pit
on a snowy day.
The challenge is not only for ordinands, but for every person
who has answered the call to serve God—to develop
on-the-job courage.
Serve with the courage of your convictions,

- not hiding behind props but standing on the promises
  of Jesus,
- not dispensing minute morsels of quick fixes but sharing
  feasts of salvation's story,

- not with manufactured emotionalism but passionate tears of joy.

Serve with ferocious fortitude—until sinners run asking what must I do to be saved,

- always faithful to the text,
- living out the Word in actions and words,
- believing that the Lord will make the way,
- always speaking the truth in love.

Serve with indefatigable intrepidity—with all you heart,
all your soul, all your strength and all your mind.
Serve with the courage of your convictions,
letting nothing and nobody turn you around.
Serve with assiduous assurance—without fear, apology,
or manipulation—
until everyone knows that Satan is a liar,
until the wicked cease from troubling and the weary are at rest,
until all the graves open up and all our dead places are revived.
Serve with sapient spirit——until Pentecost is every day;
until the blind see, the lame walk, the deaf hear, and the
dumb talk;
until darkness gives way to light;
until the lonely feel love, the diseases get well, the captives get
parole, the houseless have homes, and the naked get clothes.
Serve with visionary valor—
until everyone, everywhere knows that Jesus is real and
God is alive
until all the so-called "nobodies" realize that they are
"somebodies" in God's sight
until pretenders to the throne sit down and shut up.
Serve with nuanced nerve—
until those that study war beat their weapons of mass
destruction into tools for cultivating peace

with a weary throat until all the world knows about the blessed
hope
until every knee bows and every tongue confesses that Jesus
Christ is Lord
knowing that the devil even in the pit of hell cannot stop,
block, or top the Word of God
running with horses and through swollen rivers.
Serve with on-the-job courage—until you reach that place where
you can join your call with all who have come before you.
God is laying hands on you right now: Step into the pit.
God is anointing our heads with oil right now: Kill the lions.
God is cleaning our wounds even on a snowy day.
God is anointing your work, branding you with God's saving
grace.
God has already prepared the places where our lives as
ministers will prosper.
Do you have the courage to go when God says go, where God
says go, for as long as God says go, to whomever God says
to meet?
Can you serve with courage?
Serve with courage.
Serve with courage.

MOTHER WIT AND SISTAH SENSE

Reverend sister girlfriend, listen to what they never tell you in
seminary or the church—Mother Wit and Sistah Sense truisms,
musings, and lessons for swimming with sharks and reaching
shore:

1. Your gender is not an automatic limitation, liability,
   punishment, asset, advantage, or reward. Remember high
   school science.

2. The beauty of the journey often lies below the surface.

3. God has provided more than enough for you to make it.
   Depend more on God's grace, direction, and mercy and

less on humanity's hoops, steps, and hastily constructed barriers.

4. Some things are so ridiculous all you can do is laugh. It's a great stress releaser.

5. Remember you can never defend a lie. Truth, however, will eventually rise and outlast it.

6. Avoid any relationship where you have more to lose than the other person.

7. In a confrontation, walk away before you reach that preconversion moment of uncontrolled behavior and virulent language. People tend to penalize women more heavily than men for missteps in behavior. They may be able to recount the minute details of our actions whether they were present or not.

8. Survey the water for depth. If you are not ready to swim, stay out of the water.

9. Plan your escape route prior to entering shark-infested waters.

10. Folk proverb says, "Every shut eye ain't sleep, every good-bye ain't gone." Not everyone who looks like a shark is out to harm you. Sometimes the greatest danger comes from the remora.

11. There are negative and positive consequences for standing up for your beliefs. At least you will still recognize yourself when the battles are over.

12. Keep your eyes on the shore. Some days you will swim with ease, other days you will tread water, and some days you will just avoid the riptides.

13. Your grandmother was right. Hold your head up and always look people in the eyes.

14. People can smell fear and attack because you seem defenseless. Why are you afraid?

15. When there is blood in the water, know when to say when.

16. Remember you are not the first or only one in ministry waters.

17. It's lonely at the top and at the bottom. Swim in schools or at least pairs.

18. Take responsibilities for your own mistakes. Learn from them.

19. Avoid being an unwitting contributor to your own demise.

20. If you choose to confront the powers that be, make sure you have done your homework.

21. Attend meetings, conferences, and seminars not just to be seen but to gain useful first-hand information.

22. Knowledge is power. Learn all the rules. Use them appropriately.

23. Do not make unsubstantiated charges of prejudice unless you are certain that is the root cause of the issue. Name the evil when you are certain of its presence.

24. All of life is a process. Try not to circumvent it just for expediency's sake.

25. My mother used to say, "Just because everyone else is doing it does not mean you have to do it. Stand on you own two feet."

26. If someone constantly tells you what they can do for you, ask about the cost. Even a free lunch justifies tipping the wait staff.

27. Only you can decide if you are the bait, the target, or collateral damage.

28. Never give all your secrets, skills, or tools away to anyone for any reason.

29. My grandmother used to say, "Two wrongs don't make a right." Avoid making others pay for what someone else did to you.

30. Should you become overwhelmed, don't be afraid to call for the lifeguard.

I can hear the water churning. Keep your eyes and ears open. Try not to panic. Stop thrashing around in the water. You were built for endurance. Slow and steady is often better than quick and exhausting. This ministry thing is a marathon, not a sprint. You are doing just fine. Remember to breathe, emptying the polluted and consuming the right energy source. Can you feel God's protection enveloping you? Do you discern God's buoyant love keeping you afloat? You are almost there. Remember that little celluloid fish and keep swimming. If you need a hand, other sisters are waiting on shore.

See you in the locker room,
T

EPILOGUE

SISTER HELP

To all my sisters who need a little help,
"God will show up and will show out," "We serve a God of somehow," "God will make a way out of no way," "Don't you know God
is able?" "After while it will all be over"—these are faith statements
that have reverberated from African American churches for hundreds
of years. They speak to the belief that no matter what is going on, no
matter how bad situations seem to be, or what the so-called powers
that be have in mind, there is a God who is able to deliver, to right
wrongs, and to save. Hope is an expectation that life will change for
the better. While troubles, difficulty, ostracism, or pain continue, the
church community sayings remind us that though joy, inclusion, or
healing are not yet a reality, they will soon come. Hope means that,
although we encounter societal ills such as racism, sexism, ageism,
militarism, classism, materialism, or even academic elitism, there will
ultimately be an equitable resolution, a healing, a change, a sense of
empowerment for the better. W. Paul Jones writes that the truth of
one's faith perspective as a Christian is its livability, tested in the
midst of a supportive and accountable faith community.[1] It is the duty

---

1. W. Paul Jones, *Worlds within a Congregation: Dealing with Theological Diversity* (Nashville: Abingdon Press. 2000), 36.

of those who have experienced abundant life, who know about God, who believe in God's promises to work to help liberate others to share the good news with the captives and to help build new communities.

My life is not perfect. I have miles to go before I sleep. I have tried to share little bits of information that I have gathered over the past twenty-five or so years specifically and over my fifty-six years in general. The sum of the matter is that there is help for those who feel like they have lost their very mind and cannot find the word to say what is going on inside. We are spiritual, emotional, intellectual, and corporeal beings who are not perfect but are trying to live out our calls. We cannot do it by ourselves. There are women and men who have walked this way before and in most instances are ready to help us. Yes, there will be obstacles. But if we keep focused on the goal we will make it—perhaps bloodied, but alive and ready to do God's work.

Reverend sister girlfriends, thank you for letting me share just a little bit of what God has shown me these past few years. Some of the truisms they will never tell you in seminary or church are just common sense. Others were taught to me by life or by those I love and trust. When you have a chance, add others to the list and pass them on to help and encourage other sisters. Remember, living faith is developed in community. Until I meet you face to face, just hold on. God is working it out.

> Your sister in God's creation,
> Teresa

BIBLIOGRAPHY

Atkinson, Clarissa W., Constance H. Buchanan, and Margaret R. Miles, eds. *Shaping New Vision: Gender and Values in American Culture.* Ann Arbor: UMI Research Press, 1987.

Carpenter, Delores. *A Time for Honor: A Portrait of African American Clergywomen.* St Louis, Mo.: Chalice Press, 2001.

Chaves, Mark. *Ordaining Women: Culture and Conflict in Religious Organizations.* Cambridge, Mass.: Harvard University Press 1997.

Clark Hine, Dorothy, Elisa Barkley Brown, and Rosalyn Terborg Penn, eds. *Black Women in America: An Historical Encyclopedia, Vol. 1.* Bloomington and Indianapolis: Indiana University Press, 1994.

Cooper, Anna Julia. *A Voice from the South by a Colored Woman from the South.* Xenia, Ohio: Aldine, 1892; New York: Oxford University Press, 1988.

Dodson, Jualynne. *Engendering Church: Women, Power, and the A.M.E Church.* Lanham, Md.: Rowman and Littlefield, 2002.

Fry Brown, Teresa. *God Don't Like Ugly: African American Women Handing on Spiritual Values.* Nashville: Abingdon Press, 2000.

_____. *Weary Throats and New Songs: Black Women Proclaiming God's Word.* Nashville: Abingdon Press, 2003.

Giddings, Paula. *When and Where I Enter: The Impact of Black Women on Race and Sex in America.* New York: William Morrow, 1984.

Lindley, Susan Hill. *You Have Stept Out of Your Place: A History of Women and Religion in America.* Louisville, Ky.: Westminster John Knox Press, 1996.

Massey, James Earle. *The Burdensome Joy of Preaching.* Nashville: Abingdon Press, 1998.

Noren, Carol. *The Woman in the Pulpit.* Nashville: Abingdon Press, 1991.

Richardson, Marilyn, ed., *Maria W. Stewart, America's First Black Woman Political Writer.* Bloomington: Indiana University Press, 1987.

Townsend Gilkes, Cheryl. *If It Wasn't For The Women: Black Women's Experince and Womanist Culture in Church and Community.* Maryknoll, N.Y.: Orbis, 2001

Wessinger, Catherine, ed. *Religious Institutions and Women's Leadership: New Roles inside the Mainstream.* Columbia: University of South Carolina Press. 1996.